STROUD
AND THE FIVE VALLEYS
From Old Photographs

With many thanks
Howard

HOWARD BEARD

AMBERLEY

First published 2019

Amberley Publishing
The Hill, Stroud
Gloucestershire, GL5 4EP

www.amberley-books.com

British Library Cataloguing in Publication Data.

A catalogue record for this book is available from the British Library.

ISBN 978 1 4456 8583 0 (print)
ISBN 978 1 4456 8584 7 (ebook)

Typesetting by Aura Technology and Software Services, India.
Printed in the UK.

Contents

Introduction

4

1.   Homes, Shops and Hostelries

6

2.   Churches

22

3.   Industrial Buildings

30

4.   Transport

40

5.   Occupations

56

6.   Events

65

7.   Children

83

8.   Rural Life

87

9.   The Landscape

91

Acknowledgements

96

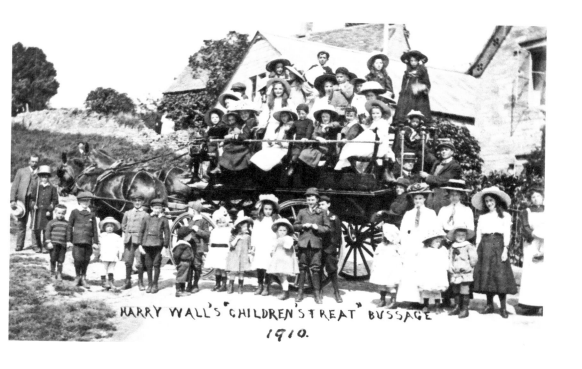

HARRY WALL'S "CHILDREN'S TREAT" BUSSAGE
1910.

Introduction

Images from the past fascinate us. They reveal the backdrop to the world our ancestors inhabited and record the changes that have taken place to towns and landscape over decades. Early photographs appear to be of equal interest to newcomers and to those whose memory takes them back, at least partially, to the scenes the pictures show.

Change is inevitable. The purpose of this book is to record Stroud and nearby villages as they were a century or so ago, not to pass judgement on whether the local physical and social environment has altered for better or for worse. Readers will form their own opinions although, in some cases, the answer is obvious: a row of sixteenth-century almshouses must surely be preferable to a few car parking spaces and an art deco cinema to a shopping mall.

In Britain we are fortunate to have so many images from the Edwardian period, as opposed to previous decades. This is due to the General Post Office deciding in 1902 that the whole of one side of a postcard could be used for a picture. Prior to this the address it was being sent to occupied one side, with the message and illustration having to share the other. This doubling of space for the photograph led immediately to a huge increase in the production of postcards all over the country. The golden age of the picture postcard was born and enthusiasm for it continued unabated for the next decade or so, with most families preserving both used and unused cards in albums. This, of course, has resulted in the creation of so much valuable pictorial evidence of life in the first part of the last century.

The Stroud area has been blessed with many significant domestic, religious and commercial buildings. Several are recorded here. But much more than just buildings has altered. Transport has changed beyond recognition. Horse buses and early motor vehicles intrigue us because they are so alien to our present-day experience. Steam locomotives, still remembered by those born before the 1960s, often provoke strong feelings of nostalgia and, for some, the need to visit one of the country's preserved railways. Likewise a trip on a canal boat – especially one powered by steam – offers an enjoyable leisure experience although, for our ancestors, such vessels were a means of earning their livelihood rather than passing a pleasant summer afternoon.

Then there are the many occupations that a hundred years or so of progress have rendered obsolete: delivering bread by donkey, horse-drawn fire appliances, gardeners using lawnmowers pulled by animals, or policemen on point duty at the Town Time in Stroud.

Neither are the events that brightened or saddened the lives of our forebears overlooked. Many have been discontinued, or altered out of recognition: Empire Day, visits to Stroud of the County Agricultural Show, May Day festivities, the Great Pageant of 1911, carnivals, the royal visit of 1922, early cinema shows, crowded election scenes, fires, floods and funerals are all covered in this book.

What is especially noticeable from old photographs, particularly of the period before the First World War, is the immense effort people put into making local and national events memorable. We see lavishly decorated streets, impressive carnival floats and busy coronation festivities. We also glimpse children at play, enjoying the rural pastimes that flourished in a pre-computerised age. At a time when disease was prevalent and educational and travel opportunities limited, old photographs still suggest a settled, organised community where people enjoyed life.

It will become apparent to the reader that some images included in the book might fit into more than one chapter. For example, should the Chalford delivery boy be located under 'occupations' or 'rural life'? Their placement is inevitably somewhat arbitrary.

Finally, it should be said that compiling this book has been a rewarding experience and it is hoped that opening a window onto a past age may convey some of this pleasure to the reader.

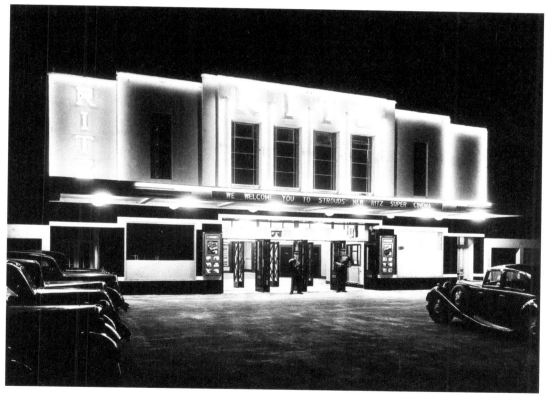

The Ritz Cinema

One of the major changes to Stroud, well remembered by older Stroud residents, resulted from the extensive fire in the summer of 1961 that destroyed the popular Ritz Cinema. The building was situated where the Merrywalks Shopping Centre now stands.

Homes, Shops and Hostelries

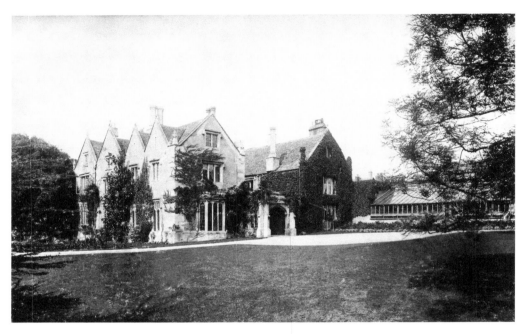

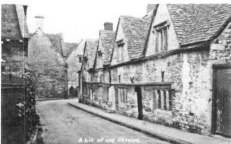

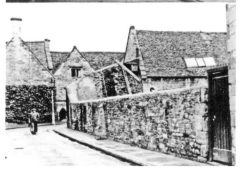

Above: Ebley Court

This fine building was either built, or rebuilt, for Thomas Bennett in 1587. Subsequently it had a fairly chequered history, receiving many alterations and additions in Tudor style. By the mid-twentieth century it was being used as a hotel. However, it later became empty, was vandalised and then demolished. In my opinion, along with Stratford Abbey and the Church Street almshouses, it stands as one of the major architectural losses in the Stroud area.

Left: The Almshouses Church Street, Stroud

These ancient and attractive almshouses were very much a feature of old Stroud, but had fallen into disrepair by the time of the Second World War. In fact the roof had already gone. Demolition took place in the mid-1960s, according to a lady who once lived in Church Street. The site is now a car park. One photograph shows the almshouses around 1910, the other what remained shortly before demolition.

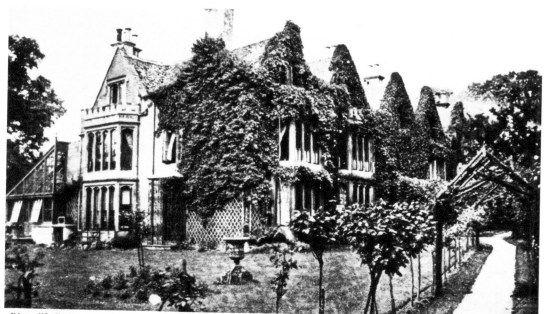

Photo W. F. Lee.   Published by James Lee, High Street, Stroud.   STRATFORD ABBEY, STROUD.

Stratford Abbey, Stroud

This fine Tudor-style edifice stood on the south side of Stratford Road close to Stratford Mill. In the mid-nineteenth century it belonged to mill owner John Biddell. From 1870 until 1939 the building housed a private school for girls, which was run by the Misses Isacke. During the Second World War it was home to a film animation company before being demolished in 1961. The site is now occupied by Tesco's petrol station.

A Pupil's Certificate Stratford Abbey College was keen to enter pupils for external examinations. Ruby Alcock was placed in the Royal Drawing Society's honours division in 1924 for her work at the college.

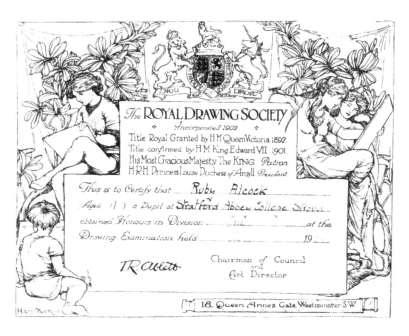

7

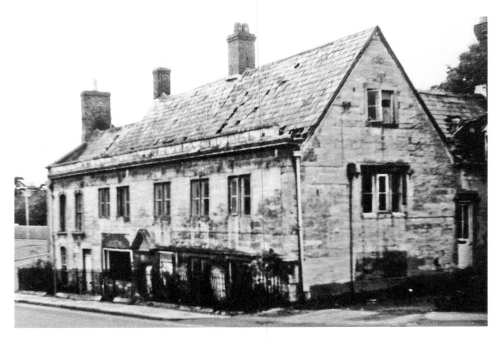

Cuttle's Mill House Wallbridge, Stroud

An architecturally significant building, the mill house was erected in the sixteenth century and refronted in classical style by John Cole in 1714. In the latter part of the eighteenth century the mill to which it belonged was a dye house and, many years later, a grist mill. The house was demolished around 1970. Its attractive shell cupboards were saved and are now preserved in the Museum in the Park. The photograph was taken by the late celebrated artist and cartoon animator Harold Whitaker, who died in 2013.

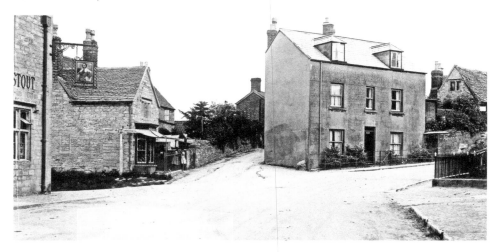

Houses at Rodborough

On the extreme left of the picture stands the Prince Albert pub. Beyond it – at the entrance to Butterrow Lane – is a shop that once housed Rodborough Post Office. This no longer exists, and neither does the symmetrical property on the right, with its twin dormers. The image is taken from a postcard franked in 1925, the work of Rodborough photographer William Adams.

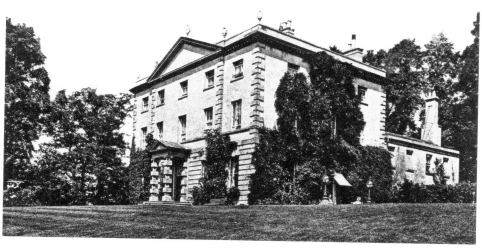

Farmhill Park, Stroud

Built around 1784 by Richard Cooke, Farmhill Park passed via the Wyatt family to J. G. Strachan in 1870. He occupied it until his death in 1892. It was later the home of Stroud's Liberal MP Charles P. Allen, who held the seat from 1900 to 1918. The house was demolished in the 1930s. The site of the building, a good example of the ornate classical style, is now occupied by Archway School.

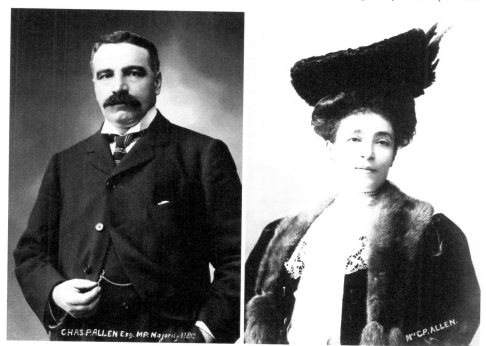

The Allens

The photograph of Mr Allen, taken to mark his election victory over Conservative candidate Cecil Fitch, was by Stroud photographer Henry Comley. The picture of his carefully attired wife is by the same photographer and was probably taken concurrently.

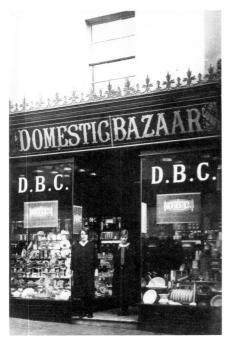

The Domestic Bazaar Company, Stroud
Situated at No. 22 King Street, this shop sold a wide
variety of household objects, as its name suggests.
The business was established in Stroud some time just
before the First World War and closed just before the
Second. On the right in the doorway is shop girl Violet
Pearce, born in Almondsbury in 1899. She later moved
to Stroud where her uncle ran a blacksmith's business.
Violet lived to be almost ninety-nine.

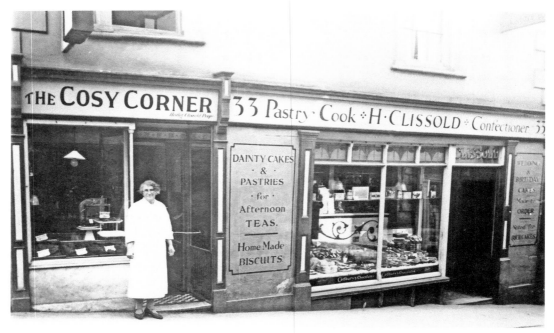

Hedley Clissold Pastry Cook, Stroud
Established somewhere around 1912, Hedley Clissold's shop survived until at least the Second World
War, possibly later. It was located at No. 33 High Street. The teashop area of the business was rather
quaintly called 'The Cosy Corner' and here his cakes, pastries and home-made biscuits would be
consumed by those Stroud inhabitants sufficiently well off at the time to afford such indulgences.

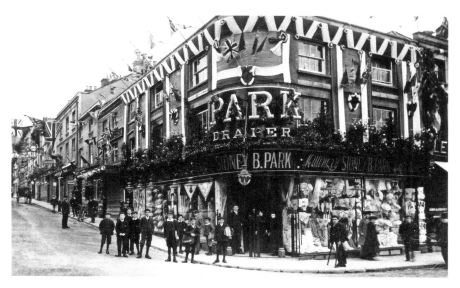

Sidney Park Draper, Stroud

Sidney Beynon Park opened his drapery business around 1895. His main premises, seen here, were on the corner of George Street and King Street, although he had a second shop at No. 5 High Street. The photograph depicts the former, possibly decorated to celebrate a visit to Stroud of the County Agricultural Show in 1907. The building was demolished around 1920 and replaced by the Midland Bank, now the HSBC.

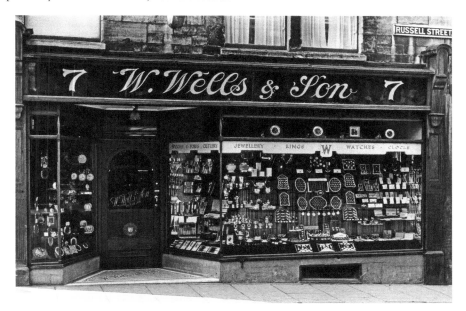

Walter Wells Jeweller and Watchmaker, Stroud

Originally from Warwickshire, Walter Wells arrived in Stroud in the 1880s. His first shop was at No. 5 Middle Street, where he described himself purely as a watchmaker. Around 1900 he moved to a more central and prestigious site at No. 7 Russell Street. By the late 1930s he was selling a much wider range of products, as his shop window shows.

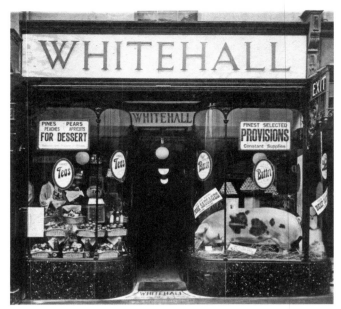

Whitehall's Grocers, Stroud
Arthur Whitehall's grocery
business was established around
the time of the First World War
and, like draper Sidney Park, by
the late 1920s he had two shops
in the town: No. 2 King Street
and No. 30 High Street. Kelly's
1931 directory describes him
rather grandly as a 'provision and
cooked meat merchant and bacon
curer'. We are fortunate in having
a picture of the front of one of
his shops. Note the pig in the
window!

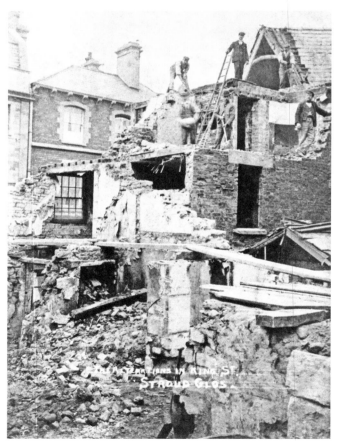

Alterations in King Street,
Stroud
From Victorian times Charles
Burghope Gardner ran a hatter's
business on the corner of King
Street and High Street. In 1905
his and other buildings on
this site were demolished and,
after temporarily moving into
alternative premises, Mr Gardner
moved back into a new shop in
the same place. This rare image
shows demolition in progress.
Nowadays Health and Safety
regulations would certainly
have something to say about
the precarious position of the
demolition workers.

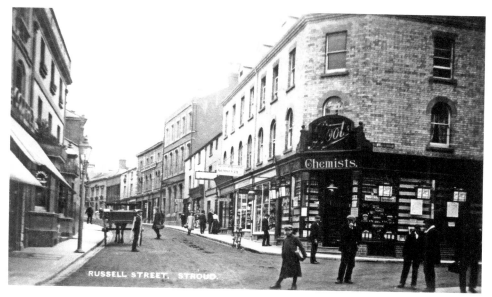

Boots the Chemists, Stroud

Situated at the corner of Russell Street and Station Road, this building housed one of the town's principal chemists. The edifice remains, but the shopfront with its decorative corner arch has gone and the store has moved to premises in the High Street. Back in the 1950s Boots contained a sit-on weighing machine, operated by the redoubtable Eileen Halliday, celebrated as the lady who refused to surrender her Dudbridge home when Sainsbury's supermarket was being built.

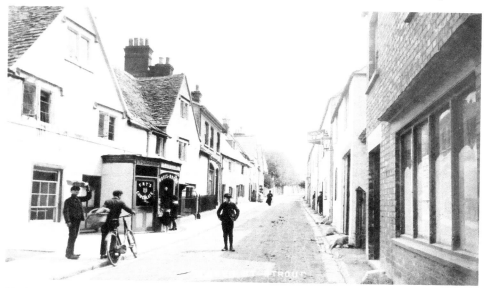

Tuck's Bakery, Lower Street, Stroud

George Tuck's bakery is listed in directories dating from just after the First World War. It was housed in a Cotswold stone building that happily survives in Lower Street. Later run by George's grandson, it ceased to trade under the Tuck name around the late 1950s when it was sold to a Cirencester firm. It is now a private dwelling.

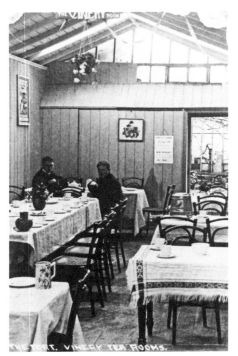

The Vinery Tearoom, Rodborough Common
This tearoom was in a wooden building within the precinct of Rodborough Fort, known in Edwardian days as Fort St George. A notice on the wall, put up by Mrs Mary Tuck who ran the business, advises customers that it is possible – no doubt on payment of a small fee – to ascend the tower and enjoy the extensive views it affords.

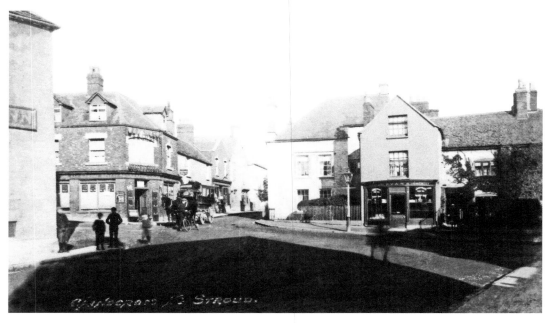

The Crossroads, Cainscross
This Edwardian postcard shows the centre of Cainscross seen from the Stonehouse direction, now with traffic lights. The White Horse Inn is on the far left, with Bridge Street leading off opposite. The right half of the image is now transformed by the disappearance of the buildings swept away around 1970 when Tricorn House was put up.

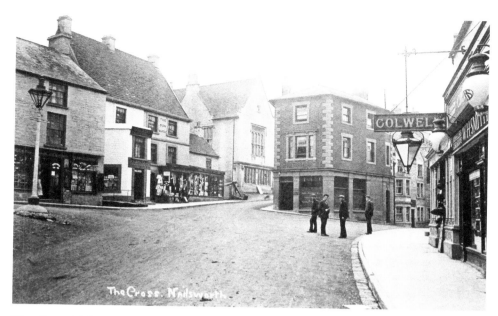

The Cross, Nailsworth

An early photograph from 1870 shows a fishmonger's at this junction in Nailsworth. By the end of the century this had disappeared to be replaced by the mainly red-brick premises of the Wilts and Dorset Bank, seen here around 1910, which in turn was demolished in 1962 to allow wider vehicular access into Market Street.

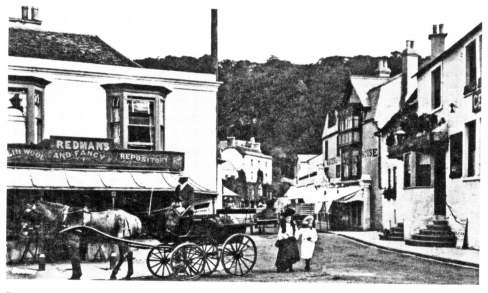

Redman's Shop, Nailsworth

At yet another crossroads, nowadays with a mini traffic roundabout, this street looks very different today. On the right is The George Hotel, which is no longer a hostelry. Mrs Mary Hephzibah Redman's grandly named Berlin Wool and Fancy Repository was replaced around 1950 by Nailsworth's clock tower.

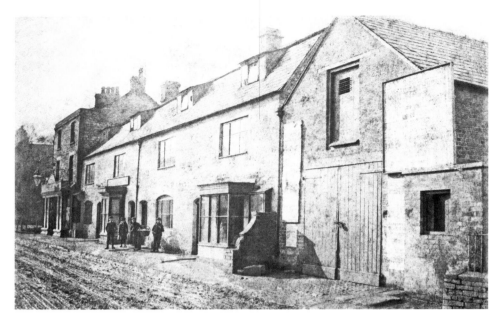

Bridge Street, Nailsworth

All the premises seen here were demolished when a new terrace of shops was put up in 1892. This photograph is personal for me since one of the new shops was occupied around 1910 by my outfitter grandfather F. W. Lee. Also, in another of these buildings, my three times great-grandmother was burnt to death in 1854, when flames from a candle she was carrying on her way to bed ignited her shawl.

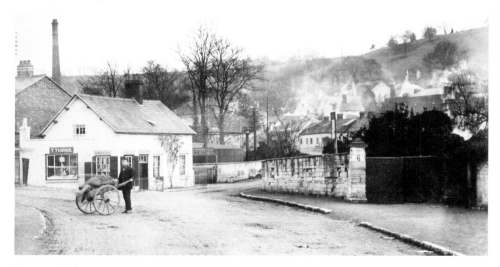

Shops at Brimscombe Corner

Access for vehicles entering London Road from Brimscombe Hill is now easier because a widened junction gives much improved visibility since the removal of several shops. This postcard by the Chalford photographer Frank Colville was produced around 1907. Businesses that have disappeared include Turner's and Thwaite's. Just to the right of these was Stephens' public weighbridge – also long gone.

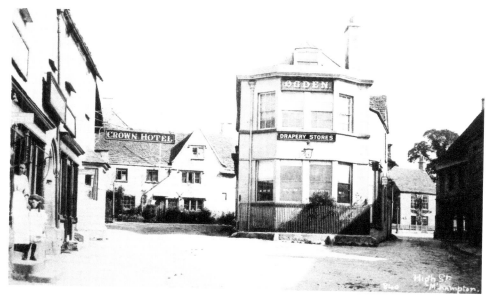

Lower Island, Minchinhampton

This postcard was franked in October 1907. On the left is F. C. Hughes' grocery store with the Crown Hotel beyond. The market house is visible on the right. Lower Island in the centre was demolished around 1920 to be replaced by the war memorial. Properties in Lower Island housed many activities over the years, including school cookery classes. There was also a rifle range in its basement. Here it is occupied by Ogden's drapery business.

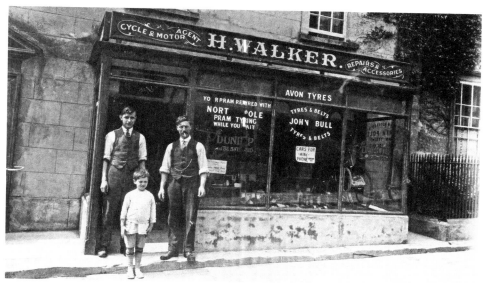

Walker's Cycle Shop, Minchinhampton

In 1919 Harry Walker's cycle business was situated in Tetbury Street. Soon afterwards he appears at a property in the High Street where he is listed by 1935 as having the phone number Brimscombe 73. A quaint advertisement in his window announces 'your pram retyred with North Pole pram tyring while you wait'.

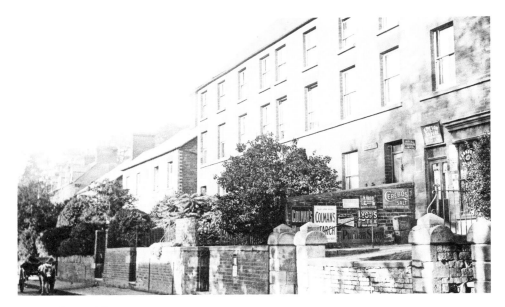

Pitson's Stores, Thrupp

This undated photograph was probably taken in the 1920s. The shop that was Mrs Elizabeth Pitson's grocery store is now a private house. Panels on the wall advertise a variety of products available within: Cerebos salt, Colman's mustard, Colman's starch, Lyons tea and three brands of soap – Hudsons, Puritan and Sunlight. At that time the building also served as Thrupp Post Office.

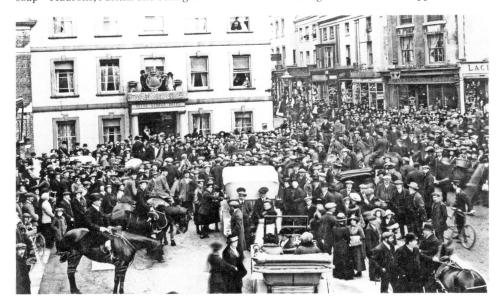

The Royal George Hotel, Stroud

Moving on to licensed premises, the Royal George was Stroud's principal inn until the Imperial Hotel opened in around 1870. This picture dates from *c.* 1910, with an unknown event taking place in front of it on King Street Parade. It closed as a hotel in 1916 when the upper floor was converted into a cinema and the ground floor became a clothing store. Demolished around 1935, it was replaced by the art deco building that stands there today.

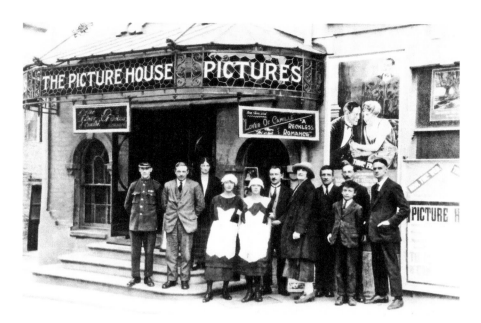

The Picture House

The cinema on the upper floor of the former Royal George Hotel was called The Picture House. Its door was roughly where the entrance to the shopping precinct is today. The photograph probably dates from the 1920s. The two men on the left could well be the commissionaire and the manager. The girls in caps and aprons are almost certainly employees. A film currently showing is *Lover of Camille, a Reckless Romance.*

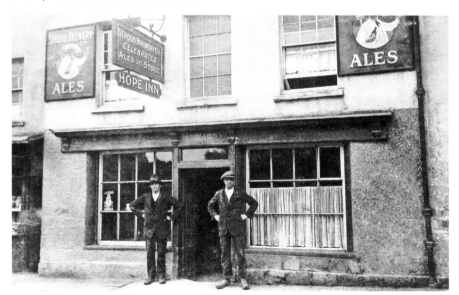

The Hope Inn, Stroud

The Hope Inn, a Stroud Brewery pub, stood in Cainscross Road opposite the then fairly narrow entrance into Merrywalks. It was demolished when extensive road widening took place around 1960 and no sign of it remains today.

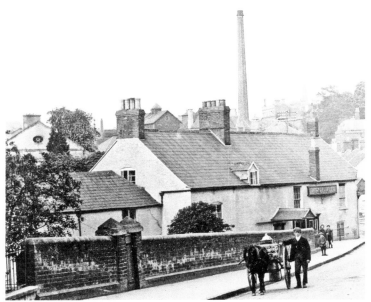

The Ship Inn, Wallbridge, Stroud Traceable back to 1820, The Ship had only a few years' working life remaining as an inn when this photograph was taken in around 1907. In 1915 my maternal grandfather Frederick William Lee took it over as a warehouse when his outfitter's business moved from Nailsworth to Stroud. Note the milk cart by the kerb and the tall brewery chimney in the distance.

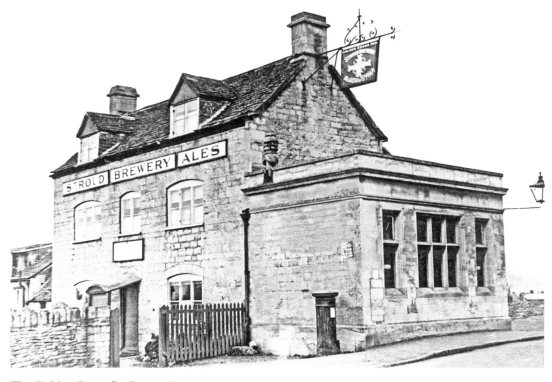

The Golden Cross, Rodborough
Now demolished, the location of this pub survives in the name of the crossroads near Stroud rugby ground. It consisted of a late eighteenth- or early nineteenth-century building with a later extension. As was the case with The Hope Inn, it was removed in order to facilitate better visibility at this busy junction.

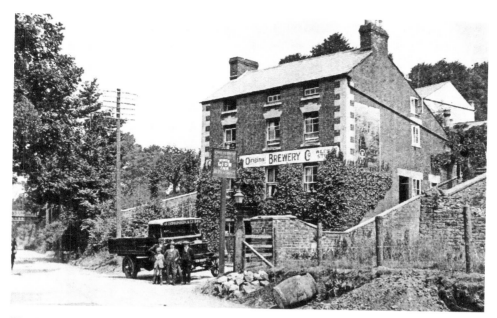

The White Lion, Lightpill

Long vanished, this pub stood close to where the road from Dudbridge meets the A46 at Lightpill. According to the sign on its wall the pub was supplied by Cheltenham Original Brewery Company, quite unusual for an inn so centrally within the area covered by Stroud Brewery.

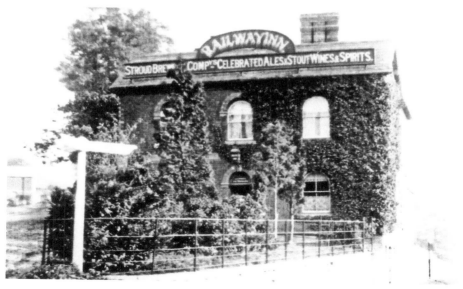

The Railway Inn, Dudbridge

The Railway Inn, named after the Midland Railway branch line that used to connect the Stonehouse & Nailsworth Railway with Stroud, stood in the angle of Dudbridge Road with Dudbridge Hill. At the time the Edwardian photograph was taken the landlord was Thomas Stephens. It was demolished in 2003 and replaced by flats.

2

Churches

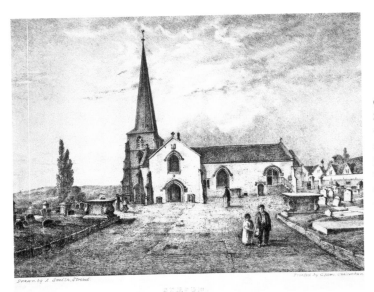

Old St Laurence Church, Stroud
Only the tower and spire remain from this medieval place of worship. Built in the early fourteenth century and originally a chapelry of the mother church at Bisley, the main part of the building was demolished in the 1860s. This print is the work of Stroud artist Alfred Newland Smith and dates from the 1830s.

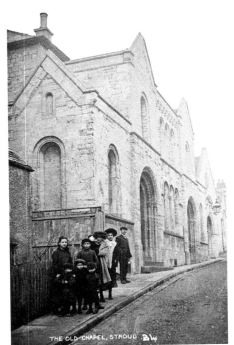

The Old Chapel, Stroud
Stroud's first Congregational Chapel was put up around 1705 in the street which came to bear its name in the upper part of the town. A second chapel of the same denomination opened in Bedford Street in 1837 in what had by then become the centre of Stroud. The two congregations amalgamated into a single church in 1970 and the Old Chapel was demolished shortly afterwards. Only the building that had been its Sunday school remains.

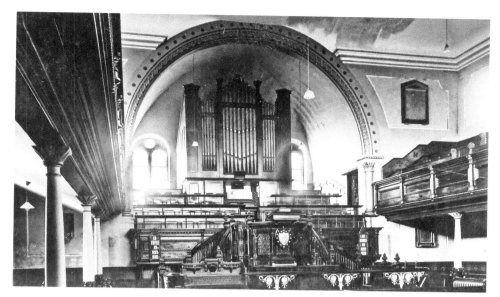

The Interior of the Old Chapel, Stroud

The interior of the Old Chapel is quite distinctive with the large arch above its organ. Of the chapel's fitments little was saved, but a memorial window to Maria Franklin, who died in 1881, survives in the Museum in the Park.

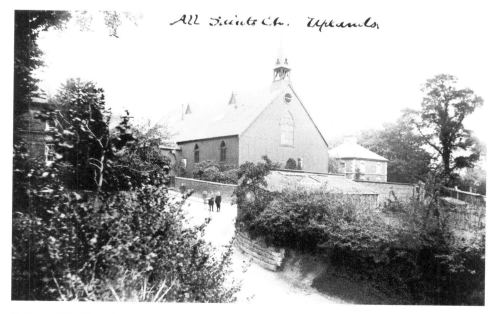

Uplands Tin Church

Before the present building was erected between 1907 and 1910 this tin church served Anglican worshippers in Uplands. So-called tin churches were actually made of corrugated iron and were obtainable in kit form, arriving by rail. They were assembled fairly quickly on-site. This tin structure's stone-built replacement was to a design by the architect Temple Moore. The tower was only added in 1932.

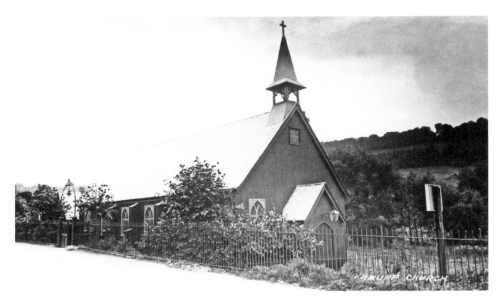

Thrupp Church

Another tin church, this building was put up as a Mission Church to Holy Trinity in Stroud in 1889. In its original form it had a thatched heather roof. It was closed in 1968 and then served as a village hall before being finally taken down in 2008 and put into storage.

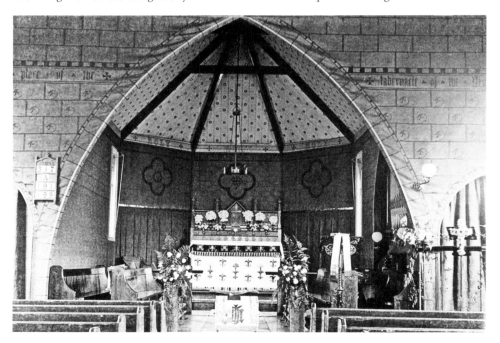

Thrupp Church Interior

Few photographs have survived of the interior of this well-loved building. This image came from the late Mrs Eunice Guy, who for many years ran the village store in the centre of Thrupp. The church's altar, pulpit and other fitments are preserved at Holy Trinity.

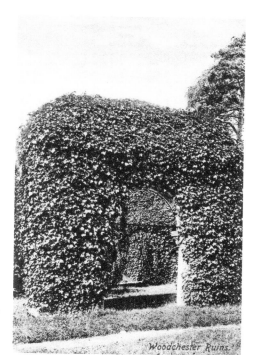

Woodchester Old Church

Woodchester's ancient church of St Mary stood near the northern boundary of the parish on the site of the great Roman villa, first excavated in the late eighteenth century by Samuel Lysons. Beneath the graveyard lies the famous Orpheus mosaic. In 1861 it was decided to erect another church on land further south. The old building was then demolished, and stone from it was used in the new construction. The Edwardian postcard shows a surviving arch of St Mary's heavily covered with ivy.

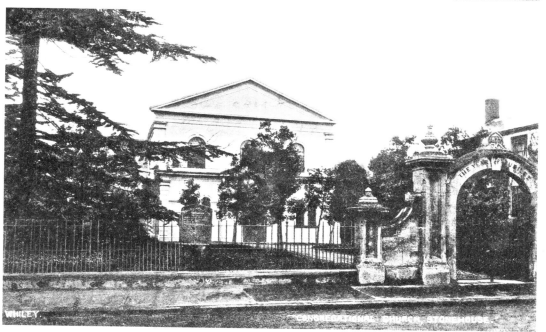

Stonehouse Congregational Chapel

This chapel was built on the west side of the High Street in 1827. During the mid-nineteenth century it reportedly had a congregation of up to 300. Services finished in 1965 and demolition followed. The area that was its graveyard is an open space today, with a few tombstones remaining.

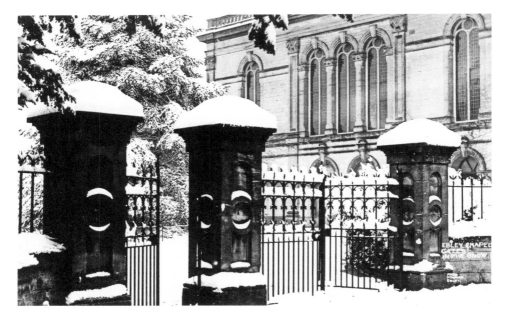

Ebley Chapel

A Countess of Huntingdon's Connection Chapel was erected in Ebley in 1798 and enlarged a couple of years later. During the nineteenth century it prospered, especially during the thirty-year pastorate of the Revd Benjamin Parsons. Ebley Chapel was rebuilt in 1881 and ceased to be used in 1967. It was taken down in 1972. This atmospheric snow view dates from around 1910.

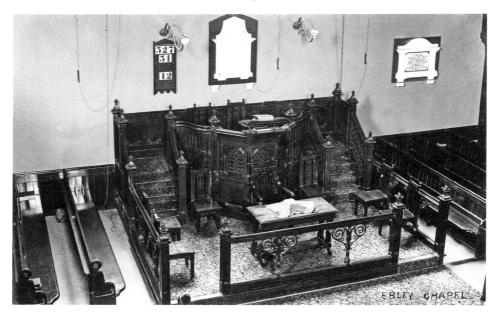

Ebley Chapel Interior

The view of the inside of the chapel again dates from the Edwardian period, during the pastorate of the Revd Robert Nott. It was taken by the Stonehouse photographer Frederick Restall and represents a typical chapel interior of a century or more ago.

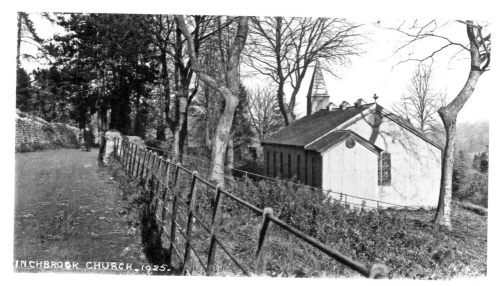

Inchbrook Church, Nailsworth

The tin church at Inchbrook was put up in 1865 and was intended to serve the Anglican cause in Inchbrook, Forest Green and Windsoredge. By the closing years of the nineteenth century it had a curate whose annual stipend was £200. The church was still standing as late as the 1970s. As the caption states, E. P. Conway of Nailsworth's photograph dates to 1925. In 1978 permission was obtained to demolish the building.

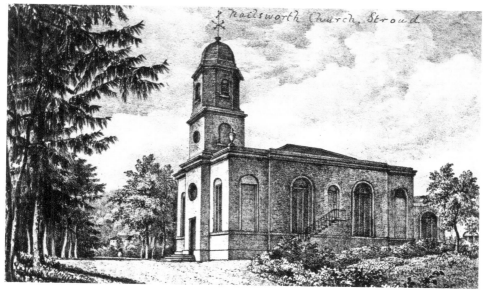

The Pepperpot Church, Nailsworth

Named for the curious top of its tower, this church was built in 1794, funded by subscription. It served as a chapel of ease to the mother church of Avening since, at that period, Nailsworth did not have parochial status. Taken down in 1898 and replaced on the same site by the present St George's, its clock was preserved and installed in a wooden tower set up on stilts nearby. It is now the clock at the bottom of Fountain Street.

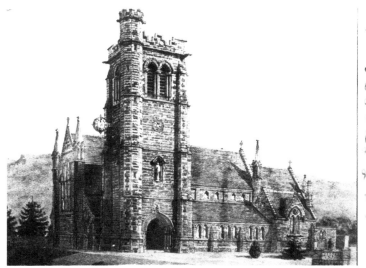

NAILSWORTH CHURCH AS IT WILL APPEAR WHEN COMPLETED.   M H REDMAN, NAILSWORTH

St George's Church, Nailsworth

This postcard, sent in 1904 by a Miss Hodges who ran a girls' private school in Bristol Road, is an interesting curiosity since it shows an architect's plan which was never fully realised. Neither the chancel nor tower was ever built owing to a lack of funds. A less complex chancel was erected in the 1930s.

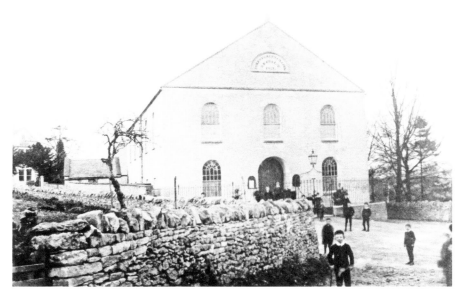

Forest Green Congregational Chapel

The first place of worship for Congregationalists at Forest Green was built in 1688 close to the present graveyard. In 1821 a second chapel was put up further down the hill at the junction of Northfields and Nympsfield roads. This is the building shown in the photograph by the Nailsworth photographer Paul Smith. The image dates from around 1900. Both chapels had gone by the early 1970s.

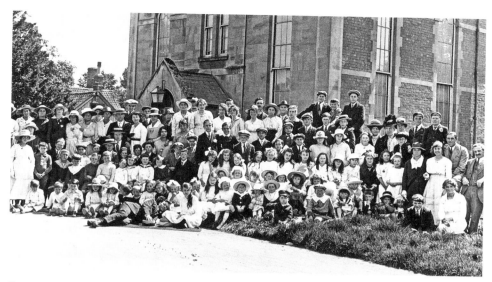

Eastington Methodist Chapel

Wesleyans put up their first building in 1808 close to the main road at Alkerton. It was reconstructed in 1870. In common with many such places of worship, by the 1960s attendance was small. It closed in 1975 and is no longer standing. The photograph shows its large congregation in 1921.

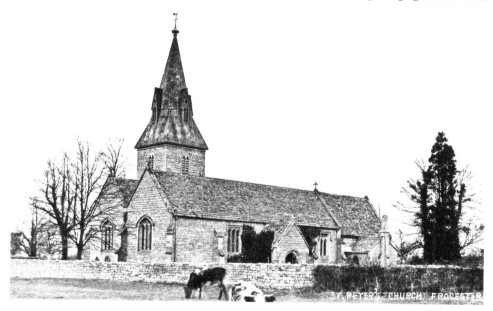

St Peter's Church, Frocester

By the late thirteenth century a church existed on this site. By the end of the 1600s a second one had been erected near the crossroads at the centre of the village. From then on, for more than a hundred years, the old parish church was used only for burials and gradually fell into disrepair. It was restored in the 1850s, from which time both churches served parishioners until 1952 when the earlier building was largely demolished. Shortly afterwards a Roman villa was excavated by the late Captain Gracie within its graveyard.

3
Industrial Buildings

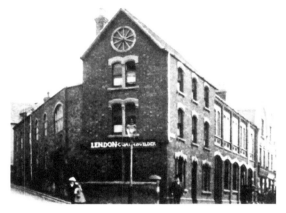

Lendon's Coach Building Firm, Stroud
Isaac Lendon opened his coach building business in the 1870s on the corner where John Street meets London Road. The firm survived until around 1920. Note the cartwheel fixed to the gable. The image dates from around 1900. The site was later occupied by Steel's Motors as a garage and showroom before demolition.

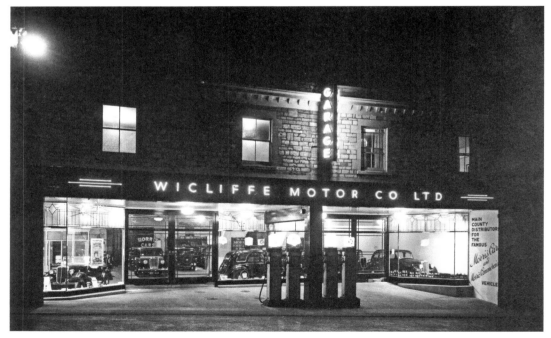

The Wicliffe Motor Company, Stroud
It surprises many people new to the area that the property in Russell Street now occupied by Peacock's store was formerly a garage. In 1897 the site was in the hands of Truscott & Sons, cycle agents. With the arrival of the motor car it became a garage and by 1914 was owned by Mr F. M. Smith, who called it the Wicliffe Motor Company. By 1927 the firm had a second garage in Cheltenham and by 1935 a service and repairs department in Cainscross Road.

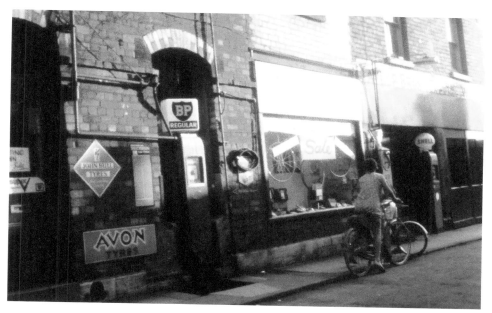

Taylor's Garage, Gloucester Street, Stroud

Taylor Brothers' business began as a bootmaker's firm on the corner of Bath Street and Gloucester Street. By the early years of the twentieth century it dealt with cycles and motor cars. The picture dates from 1966 when petrol pumps still stood at the bottom of Bath Street. Note the advertisement panels.

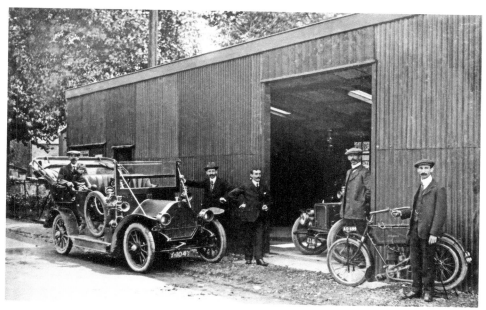

Taylor's Garage, Merrywalks, Stroud

The repairs section of Taylor's Garage was on the south side of Merrywalks. In a photograph of around 1917, William George Taylor sits in the car with his young son Lloyd. The other people, from left to right, are Archie, Ernie, Percy and Frank Taylor.

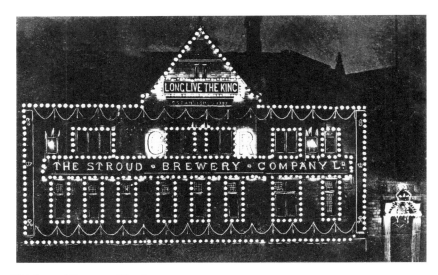

The Old Stroud Brewery Headquarters

Founded by Peter Leversage at Middle Lypiatt in 1760, the brewery moved to Rowcroft in 1793. By 1818 it was being run by Joseph Watts. On his death in 1855 the business passed to grandson Joseph Watts Hallewell. The firm amalgamated with Cheltenham and Hereford Breweries in 1957, ceased brewing in 1967 and lay empty for several years before being demolished. The site is now occupied by Ecotricity. The 1937 photograph shows it decorated for the coronation of George VI.

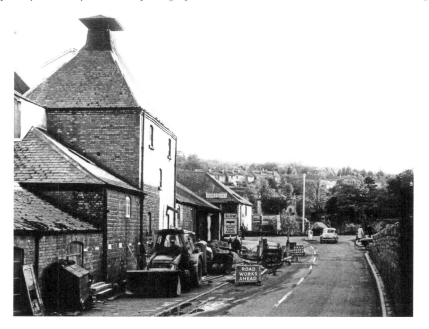

Stroud Brewery, Merrywalks Side

Taken in May 1966, this image shows the brewery buildings towards the very end of the time when the factory was active. Marion Hearfield's 2016 book about the Old Stroud Brewery states that the buildings shown include grain stores, an elevator plant, maltings (the tall structure) and the new delivery yard.

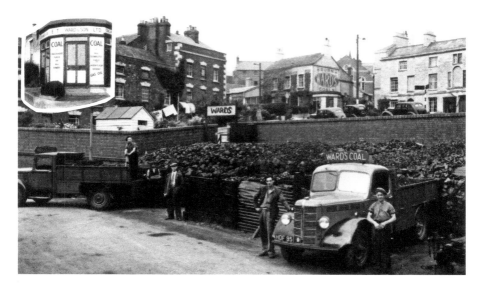

Coal Delivery, Stroud

E. T. Ward's coal business was run for many years from a yard roughly where the Brunel Mall is today. Its office was in a wooden building attached to what was then my grandfather's house on the corner of London Road with Union Street. Set into the concrete outside was a giant chunk of anthracite, well remembered by older Stroud residents. Anthracite, coal yard and office have now all gone, as have several nearby buildings. The inset shows the giant piece of coal.

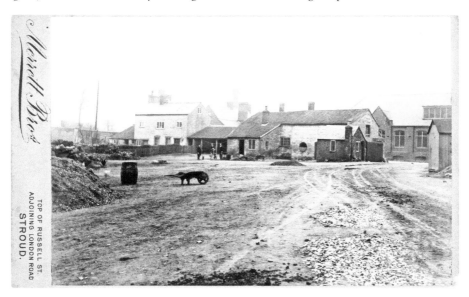

Dudbridge Wharf

This rare image was commissioned by E. T. Ward & Son from local photographers Merrett Brothers around 1900. It shows their depot on Cainscross Wharf at Dudbridge, where coal would have been offloaded from canal barges. Just visible on the right gable of the centre building is the firm's name. To the left off shot, an early crane still survives from the time when the wharf was a busy scene of waterborne freight.

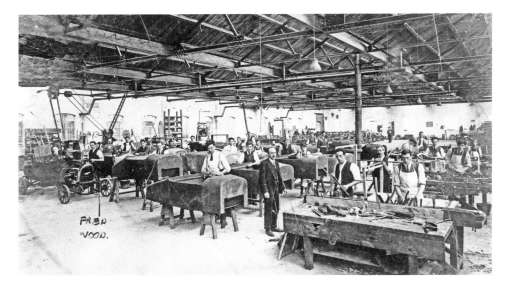

Hampton Cars of Dudbridge

Founded by William Paddon in Warwickshire before the First World War, the initial company went into receivership in 1915. In 1919 the re-established business moved to Dudbridge. Up until 1924 the firm made approximately 300 cars annually, before failing again in that year. Although Hampton Cars was refounded, production finally ceased in 1933. The photograph shows the interior of the factory, probably in the 1920s. The site is now occupied by Sainsbury's store.

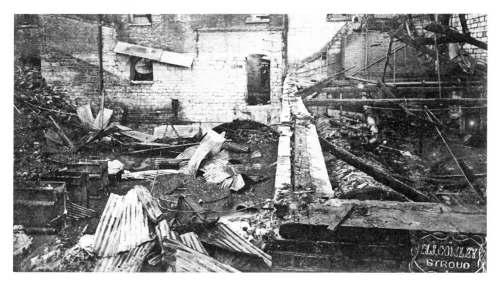

Townsend's Mill

This building, originally called Stratford Mill, was mentioned in 1607 as a fulling mill and was later owned by the Gardner family, who lived in what is now the Museum in the Park. After passing through several hands, it was sold in 1901 to R. Townsend & Son, corn, cake, seed and manure merchants. The photograph shows the aftermath of the major fire it suffered in 1908. Rebuilt, it was eventually taken over by Rank Hovis McDougall Ltd, before being closed and demolished after another fire. Its site is now occupied by Tesco's store.

Stroud Sanitary Laundry Co., Ltd.,

EBLEY, near Stroud, Glos.

This Laundry, being under the Factory Act, PERFECT SANITATION is Guaranteed.

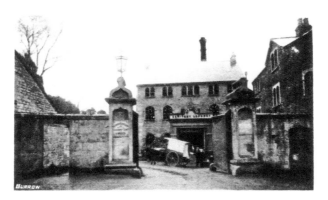

No Work of an Undesirable Kind Received.

Special Terms for Schools, Houses of Business, Hotels and Public Institutions.

NO CHEMICALS INJURIOUS TO LINEN USED.

Ebley Laundry

Established for many years in a large building, formerly part of Ebley Cloth Mills, at the point where Oil Mills Lane joins the main Stonehouse to Stroud road, this firm was one of Ebley's main employers. By the 1960s it had closed and become the warehouse for the Cainscross and Ebley Co-operative Society. Following demolition it was replaced by modern housing. The rather poor-quality picture comes from Burrow's 1903 Stroud Guide.

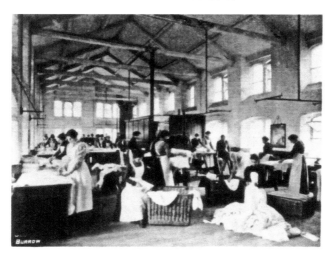

The Company's Vans Call for and Deliver Work.   Price List on Application.

All Communications respecting work, etc., to be addressed to "The Manageress."

TERMS:—CASH ON DELIVERY.

Inside Ebley Laundry

The inside of the laundry shows a scene of considerable activity and is taken from the same Stroud Guide as the previous photograph. The building was tall to accommodate high jacquard looms.

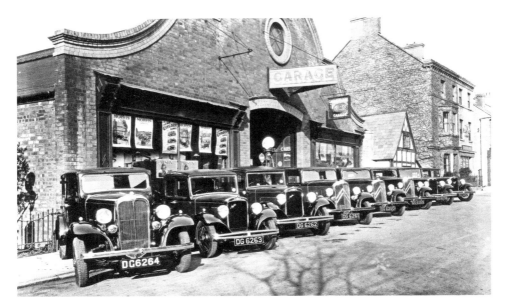

Gardiner's Garage, Stonehouse

Edwin C Peckham's photograph of Gardiner's Garage in Stonehouse High Street probably dates from the interwar period. Ted Gardiner had a cycle works in the High Street in 1900, which burnt down in 1924. At one time he also had a second garage on the Green. In 1921 he bought land next to his High Street premises and built a garage that eventually became Williams and Thomas around the 1960s. This was later demolished and replaced by the present Co-op building.

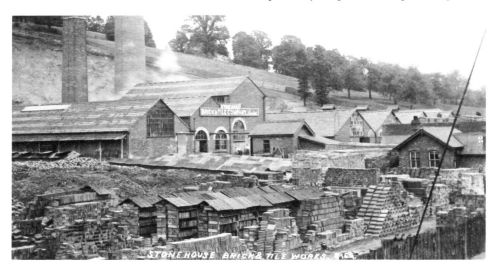

Stonehouse Brick and Tile Company

Once one of the most important firms in the local area, the Stonehouse Brick and Tile Company was established in the 1890s and has now entirely gone. It made house bricks with the firm's name stamped into them, many preserved in the Museum in the Park, and also items of terracotta and garden ornaments. Mr Alec Anderson, father of Jack Anderson, a well-known Stonehouse historian, was its first manager. Where the factory stood has since been developed for housing. The larger of its chimneys came down in October 1965.

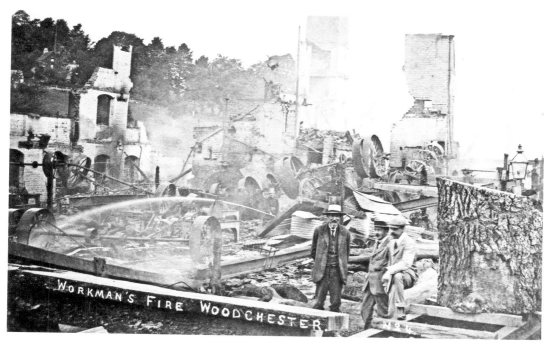

Workman's Timber Firm at Woodchester

A fire broke out in the early hours of 4 August 1911 at Henry Workman's sawmills at Woodchester. As can well be imagined with such combustible materials around, it soon developed into a raging conflagration. A member of Stroud Volunteer Fire Brigade narrowly escaped being killed by a falling wall. The site of Workman's business is currently occupied by modern industrial buildings.

Hillier's Bacon Factory, Nailsworth

This highly successful local business started in Regency times as a stall in Market Street. In 1830 the firm transferred to the hamlet of Newmarket. It became a limited company in 1865. By 1900 an extensive factory existed, which was replaced in turn by a new purpose-built one in the 1960s. After successive takeovers, the site was closed down and the buildings demolished in 1993. Housing development followed. The illustration is one of the firm's trade cards. The pig is actually a stuffed specimen and appears on several different images.

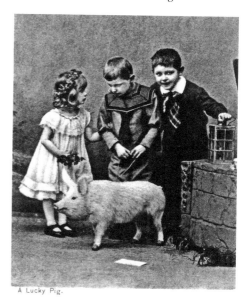

A Lucky Pig.

FROM

HILLIER'S BACON CURING Co., Ltd.,

NAILSWORTH, NEAR STROUD.

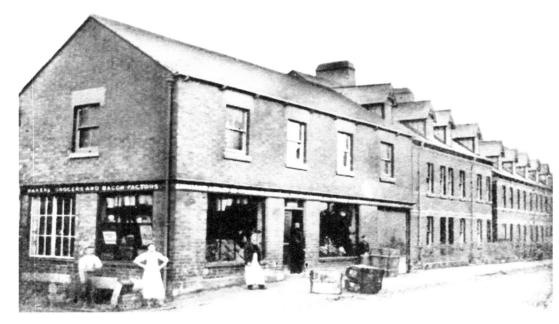

Cainscross and Ebley Co-operative Society
Founded in 1863, the society's headquarters was for many years in buildings opposite The White Horse pub at Cainscross. Extensions to its premises took place in 1888–89. Still visible on the façade are inscriptions such as 'Labour and Wait' and 'Unity is Strength'. Its golden jubilee in 1913 was celebrated with further refinements to its main building. The rather poor printed picture is from the society's 1913 jubilee book and shows the original building in 1868.

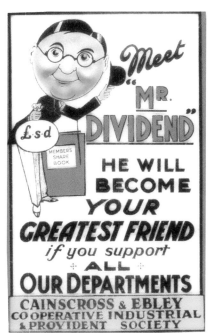

A Co-operative Society Advertisement
Taken from a set of lantern slides provided for the Co-op, probably in the 1920s, and recently acquired by Stroud Local History Society, this rather charming image reflects advertising styles of the period.

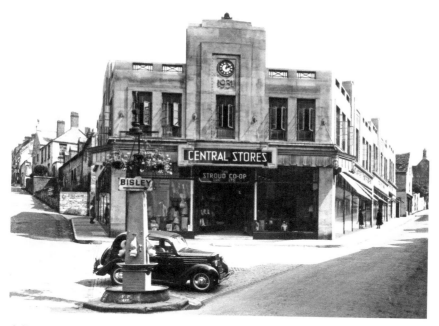

Stroud Co-operative Society

A second co-operative society was founded in Stroud in 1882. A rather damaged photograph exists of its original premises in Chapel Street. Shown here is the new 1931 headquarters building put up for the society in art deco style at The Cross. Note the fountain, one of the decorative dolphins from which is in the Museum in the Park.

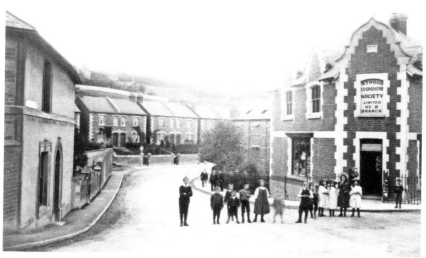

The Slad Road Co-operative Store

Just like its sister organisation, the Stroud Co-operative Society had several branches. This is number eight in Slad Road pictured around 1912. The children have been included not so much to give life to the image, but because the photographer knew their parents would buy multiple copies of the resulting postcard. Incidentally, at just about this time the manager of the shop was Reggie Lee, father of writer and poet Laurie, who was born a little further up Slad Road.

4

Transport

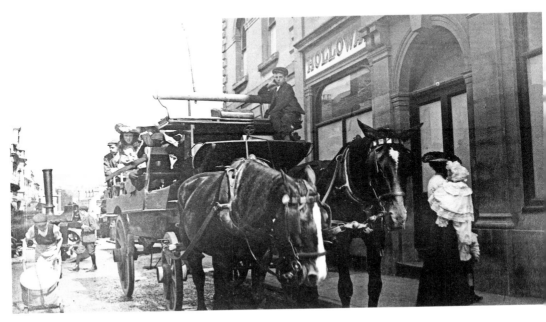

The Chalford Horse Bus
Around 1905, during the last years of horse buses in the Stroud district, a young man called Harry J. Bird
photographed them. It may be that he was simply experimenting with a newly acquired camera, or that he sensed
that an important change was about to happen and that he should record what would be lost. In this significant
and atmospheric image the Chalford horse bus waits for passengers outside what is now Bateman's Sports shop.

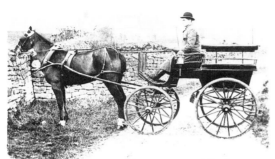

C. Niblett, Ruscombe,

Respectfully solicits your Patronage.

Moderate Charges. with Satisfaction.

An Edwardian Taxi
Horse buses did not provide adequate
coverage to all outlying villages in the
area, so a form of taxi service was
supplied by local carriers. Charles
Niblett operated such a business at
Ruscombe, transporting passengers,
and no doubt parcels and packages,
into local towns. His trade card has
survived in excellent condition.

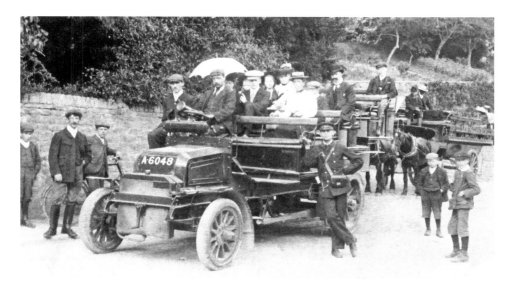

The Old and the New

This photograph, taken at the foot of Marle Hill in Chalford, is important because it records the changeover from horse-drawn to mechanically powered buses. The late Lionel Padin, an expert on the history of the Stroud area, told me that the picture dates from around March 1905. In the foreground is a London-registered Tilling-Stevens machine. Parked behind it is a horse bus run by the Townsend family.

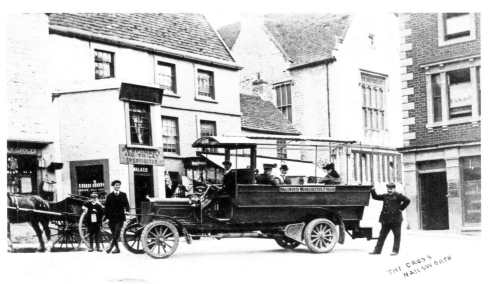

A Nailsworth Motor Bus

The bus service between Stroud and Nailsworth also became motorised in the early years of the last century. The Chalford photographer Frank Colville's picture shows one of the new vehicles at The Cross in Nailsworth. The board fixed to the side shows its route. Interestingly, side panels on early buses were detachable so that fresh air could be enjoyed by passengers during the warmer months of the year.

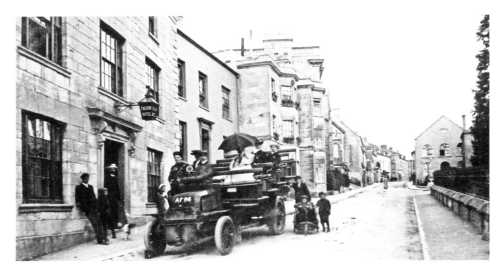

The Painswick Bus Service

The Great Western Railway opened a motor bus service to Painswick in 1905, just as they had to Chalford. Here outside the Falcon Hotel a lady shades herself from the sun with a parasol. This is one of the buses with an AF registration, brought up by rail from Cornwall. A photograph exists of such a vehicle arriving on a railway wagon at Stroud GWR station.

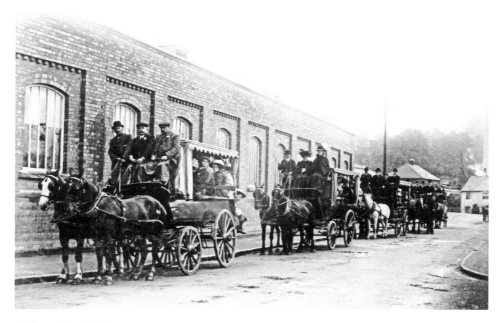

A Horse Bus Outing

A series of horse buses at Dudbridge has lined up ready to take a group on an outing. In the distance is The Bridge Inn, which stood where a roundabout exists today. On the back of the photograph is written 'Grampy Woodman from Kingscourt let out his brake and pair', so he is presumably providing one of the buses. The image from which this is copied was kindly lent by Mrs D. Martin of Bussage.

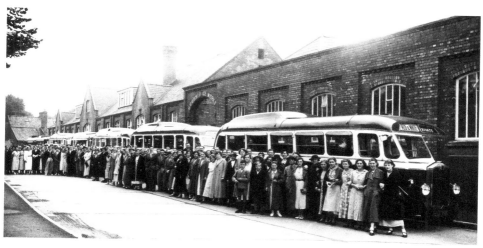

A Coach Outing

A second outing picture, taken at the same spot a generation later, is captioned 'Staff Outing Messrs Copeland Chatterson and Co Ltd, Dudbridge to Weymouth July 11 1937.' This photograph records a custom dating from the time when factory outings were common. Large numbers of employees would set off for the day, sometimes by rail, sometimes as here by coach, usually to a seaside resort.

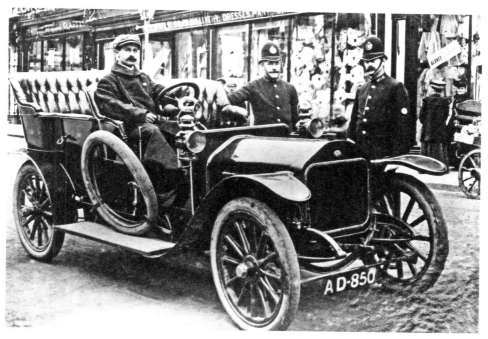

A Stroud Taxi

Here on King Street Parade, in front of Lewis and Godfrey's clothing store, is a motorist familiar in Stroud in the first half of the last century. His surname was Reed and he was known to all and sundry as Tommy. He operated a taxi service, but apparently also drove occasionally for local gentry who owned motors but did not have a full-time chauffeur. The friendly policemen were called Spicer, on the right, and Neale.

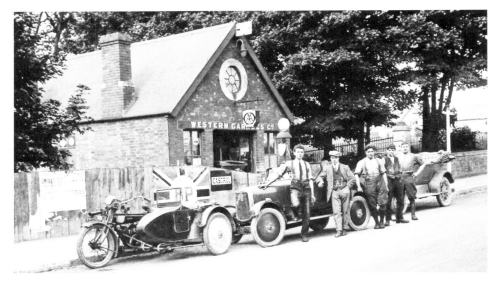

Western Garages Company

Photographed around 1926, this business was on the Cainscross side of Marling School. The firm has gone, but the structure with its distinctive round window survives today. The men are, left to right, Bill Benjamin, Sid Davis, and Harry, Leonard and Ewart Lawrence. Around the time of the First World War the Lawrences lived in what is now my house in Bisley Road. My father came to play at the property as a boy – an amazing coincidence!

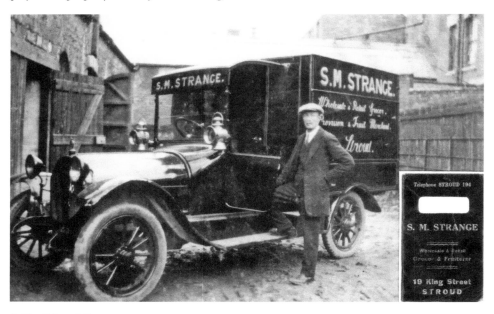

A Traditional Grocer

Strange's was a long-established grocery and greengrocery business in King Street. One reason for its decline and eventual closure in the 1960s was the arrival of Stroud's first supermarket, on King Street Parade. The photograph dates from the 1920s. As a student around 1963 I had a summer vacation job driving a later delivery van for the firm. The inset image shows a 1960s order book.

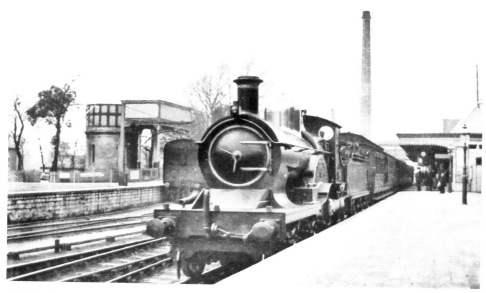

A Main-line Train at Stroud

We now move on to rail transport. As mentioned earlier, Harry J. Bird was active with his camera around 1905 capturing the last days of the horse buses. It seems he was also fascinated by railway engines. Note the original 1845 water tower to the left of the Edwardian one.

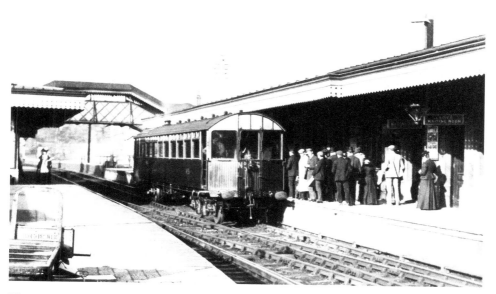

The First Railcars

In 1903, the GWR inaugurated a system of railmotors to satisfy an increasing demand for local short-distance travel through the Stroud valleys. The service was to operate from Chalford, where they were to be housed, and passengers could board at Brimscombe, Stroud and Stonehouse stations plus – importantly – intermediate halts. Railmotors cost £2,500 each, could travel at 45 miles per hour and carry fifty-two passengers. An early model is seen here at Stroud GWR station.

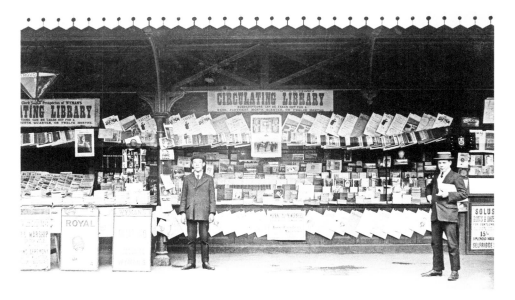

Wyman's

In 1905, W. H. Smith lost its bookstall contract with the Great Western Railway to Wyman's, which subsequently ran the business in Stroud's GWR station. This also incorporated a circulating library. The mention of warships on one of the posters suggests this is a First World War photograph. The picture came to me because a keen-eyed fellow postcard collector spotted the name Stroud on the lamp hanging top left.

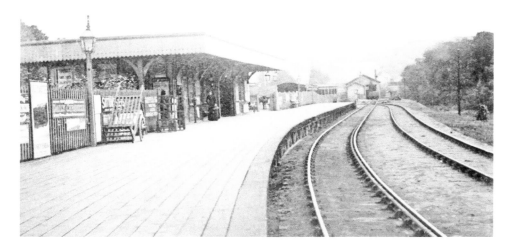

Stroud Midland Railway Station

The Midland Railway's branch line was cut through to Stroud only in 1885. The station, originally called Wallbridge, was made of wood, unlike its GWR counterpart of forty years earlier. The Bell Hotel at the lower end of Rowcroft was put up to cater for passengers arriving in the town by the Midland, just as The Imperial was for those coming by the GWR. Stroud's Midland station, track and buildings, were totally demolished when the bypass – Dr Newton's Way – was put in. The photograph was taken in the 1880s or 1890s.

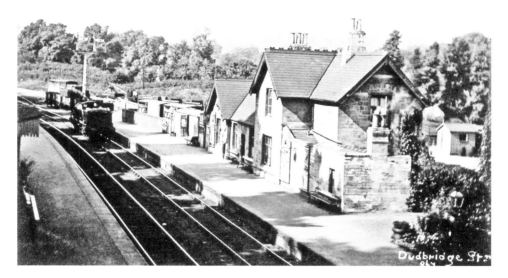

Dudbridge Station

Originally called 'Dudbridge for Stroud', this little station was built at the point on the Stonehouse to Nailsworth Midland line where the short Stroud branch diverged. As can be seen, during Edwardian times one of its subsidiary buildings was a reused railway carriage. All that remains of the station is a section of brick wall and platform by the roundabout at the bottom of Selsley Hill.

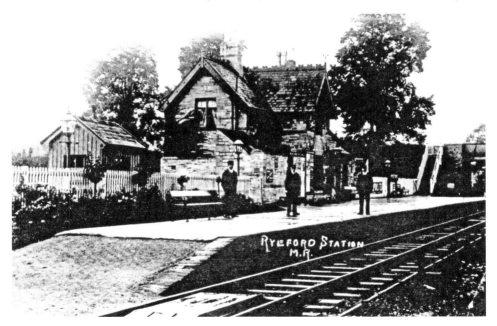

Ryeford Station

Intended to serve Ryeford, Kings Stanley and Leonard Stanley, this station on the Stonehouse & Nailsworth Railway opened in 1867. It had a two-storey stationmaster's house and sidings for the large timber yard nearby. When the Dudbridge to Stroud extension opened in 1885 a signal box was also built. The line finally closed in 1966 and the site of Ryeford station is now covered by the A419.

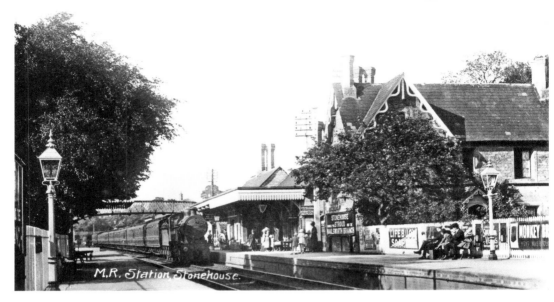

M.R. Station Stonehouse.

Stonehouse Midland Station

This station on the main London Midland Scottish line was opened on 8 July 1844. It was officially known as Stonehouse Bristol Road. Under the Beeching axe it closed to passengers in 1965 and freight the following year. Its surviving stationmaster's house is opposite the Stonehouse Court Hotel.

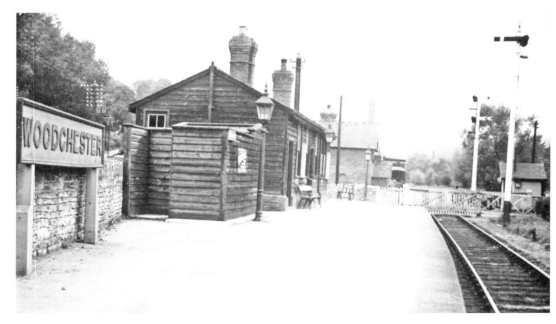

Woodchester Station

Originally built to serve both Woodchester and Amberley, this Midland branch line station has also disappeared. It stood near where the road leading down from The Ram Inn meets the A46.

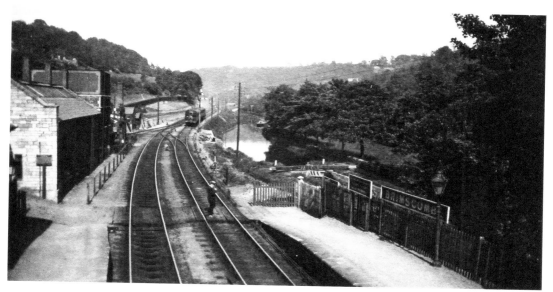

Brimscombe Station

Returning to the Great Western system, Brimscombe station opened in 1845 on what was then called the Cheltenham & Great Western Union Railway line. Its main building was on the up side. The station complex included a large goods shed, several sidings and a signal box. When demolished, part of the station site became incorporated into the A419.

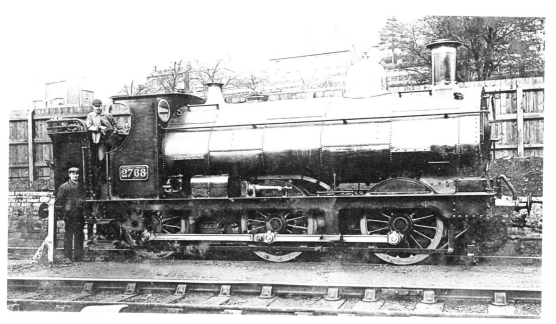

Brimscombe Bankers

Also at Brimscombe was a shed where banking engines were housed. These assisted freight and long passenger trains on the Sapperton Bank incline. The postcard image was taken around 1905. Brimscombe station closed in November 1964. The loco is an 0-6-0 saddle tank of the '2721' class.

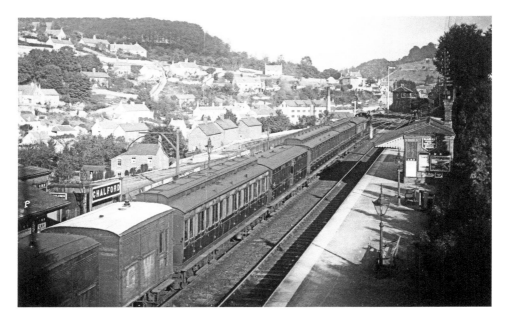

Chalford Station

When the Great Western line was opened to Gloucester in 1845 no station existed at Chalford. However, the need for one became increasingly obvious and was answered on 2 August 1897. Chalford had two platforms, a signal box, sidings, cattle pens and, at one stage, a shed for the railmotors. Just as with Brimscombe it closed in November 1964.

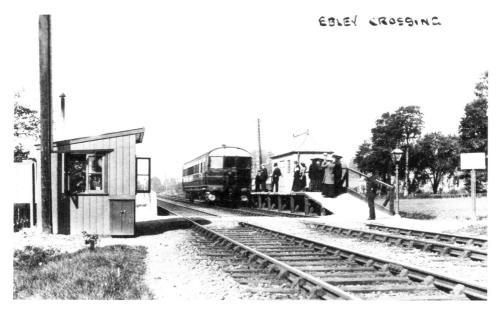

Ebley Halt

When the railmotors started to operate on the GWR line between Chalford and Stonehouse, various halts were installed between the stations. Ebley Halt, pictured around 1905 by Stonehouse photographer Frederick Restall, included a pagoda-type shelter much favoured by the company.

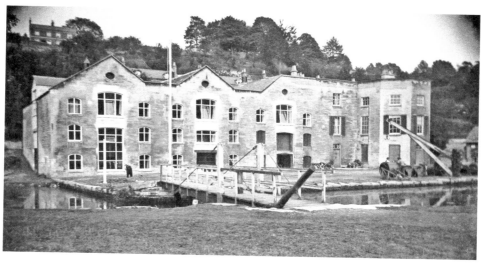

The Headquarters Building of the Thames & Severn Canal

Moving next to waterborne transport, this fine building served as headquarters and warehouse for the Thames & Severn Canal Company and was situated on the north side of Brimscombe Port basin, now filled in but due to be re-excavated as part of the current canal regeneration project. A polytechnic school existed here from 1889 to 1944. It was later the home of Brimscombe's secondary modern school, or the 'Poly' as it was nicknamed. It was demolished in 1966.

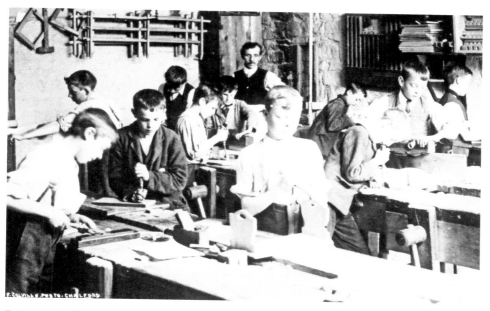

Brimscombe Polytechnic

During Edwardian days classes at the former canal headquarters were held for both sexes and were numerous and varied. By 1910 over 300 students were on roll and courses on offer included woodwork, leatherwork, embroidery, art needlework, arithmetic, bookkeeping, shorthand, typing, science, cabinetmaking, metalwork, mechanical engineering and ornamental ironwork. The posed photograph shows a woodwork class and is by Chalford photographer Frank Colville.

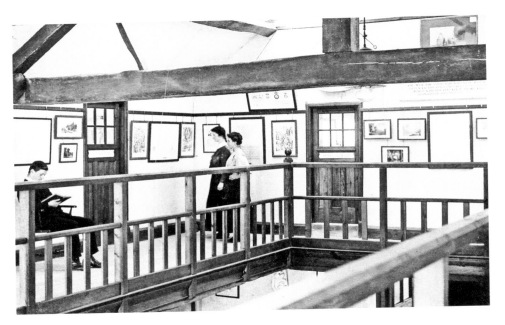

The Polytechnic Reopens

Following renovation the polytechnic reopened in 1911 and this photograph is believed to have been taken at that time. On the left is a door marked 'Advanced Art', while on the right a wall plaque promotes the advantages of acquiring an education.

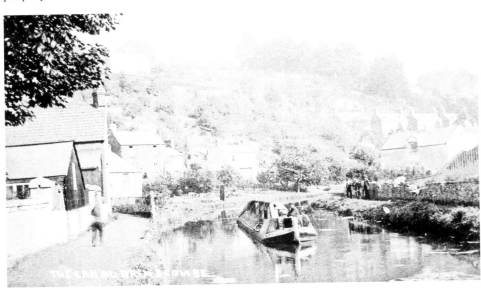

A Working Canal Barge

Photographs of working boats on the canals in the Stroud area are not common. This one shows a barge heading west on the Thames & Severn Canal near Brimscombe Corner – a part of the canal almost unrecognisable today. It is probably passing through the village on its way back from delivering coal to James Smart's wharf at Chalford. The last barge travelled through Sapperton Tunnel to the Thames in 1911.

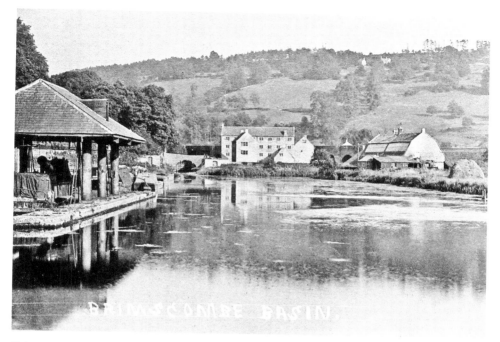

Brimscombe Port Basin

This photograph looks east across the basin. On the left is the barge-weighing machine, with the dredger *Empress* inside. Off shot to the right was an island that was used, we are told, for storing coal safely away from potential fuel thieves. One of the purposes of Brimscombe basin was to allow for the transfer of goods from Severn trows to the narrower Thames barges.

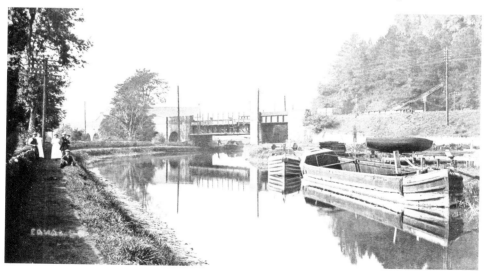

The Bourne Boatyard

To the right on this rare image is the entrance to the boat repair yard at the Bourne. Barges needing attention, or having just been repaired, are moored nearby. The position of the long-vanished yard can be gauged from where the railway crosses the canal.

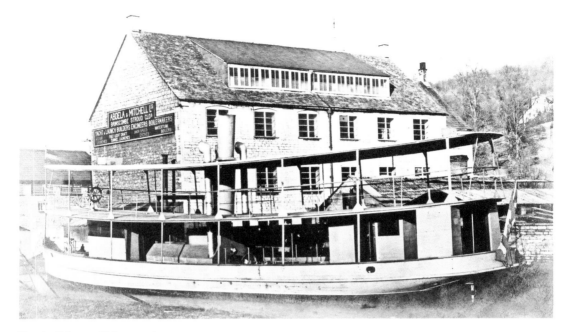

Boatbuilding at Brimscombe

Isaac Abdela's father fled from Turkish rule in Corfu in 1875 when the boy was just three months old. His Jewish family had been there since at least 1620. The Abdelas settled first in Manchester, where they prospered. Then in 1901 Isaac acquired Edwin Clark's boatbuilding business at Brimscombe. Under Isaac's management this also thrived. The photograph shows a newly launched boat and the factory on the northern side of the canal where engines were built.

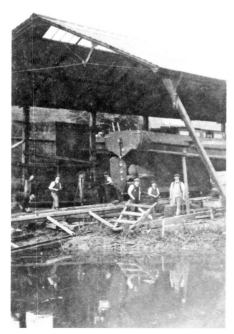

Abdela's Boatyard

This little photograph, taken in 1917, is believed to be unique. It shows a craft being built in the boatyard on the south side of the canal. Vessels built at Brimscombe were partly deconstructed in order for them to be able to pass under canal bridges. They were then floated to Sharpness and put onto ocean-going ships so as to reach their destinations in Africa, or the river systems of South America.

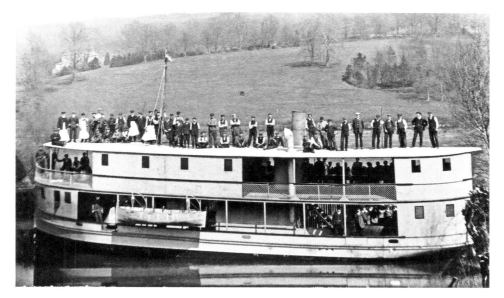

The Launching Ceremony

A finished vessel floats on the canal. Brimscombe Court is just visible in the distance. It was traditional at the launching ceremony for the workforce to assemble on top of the boat for a photograph. A local person once told me that Abdela's was a popular firm to work for: since Isaac was Jewish, employees were given both British and Jewish holidays!

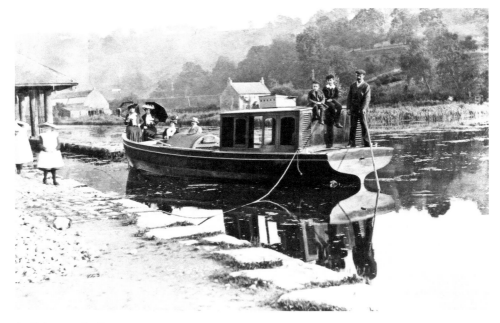

At Brimscombe Port

A final canal photograph shows a small boat next to the barge-weighing machine at Brimscombe basin. It is thought to be partially fitted out since it has a boiler, but no stack. The picture dates from 1905 and is rather charming, but the family to which it relates is not known.

5
Occupations

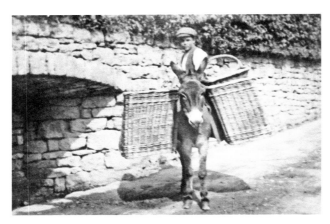

The Bread Boy, Chalford

The paths that run along Chalford's hillsides do not lend themselves easily to four-wheeled traffic. Consequently produce such as bread was delivered to cottages by donkey. As well as the two large panniers across the animal, the bread boy also had a smaller basket in which to carry loaves to doorways. This is a postcard from the collection of the late Fred Hammond, a well-known Chalford historian. A modified donkey service was recently reintroduced.

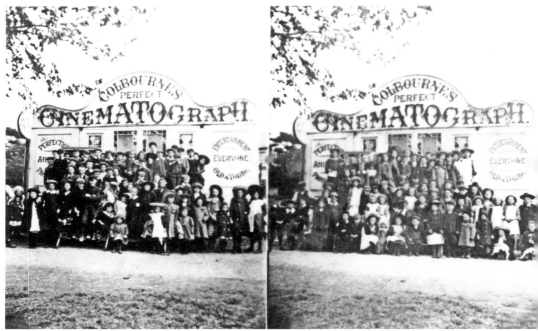

An Early Cinema Proprietor

Frank Colbourne, born in Stroud in 1861, was an important pioneer of early cinema in the area. His travelling show was running by 1900, even before the more celebrated Vincent 'Spot' Walker began his fixed-site picture house in Lansdown. At first glance the photograph looks like a stereoscopic image, though closer inspection shows it is not. Beyond the wooden façade was a marquee where attendees enjoyed Colbourne's show.

A Visiting Dentist

In Kelly's 1910 Trade Directory D. Gore Boodle (is Gore a good name for a dentist?) is listed as an 'artificial teeth manufacturer' in Gloucester. By 1919 the firm had a branch in Stroud. Their trade card makes fascinating reading: 'Extractions before 10 a.m. free' – a move to help the needy poor; 'A lady always in attendance' – no doubt to protect the modesty of female patients while being treated under gas; extractions 'without the slightest pain' – believe this if you wish!

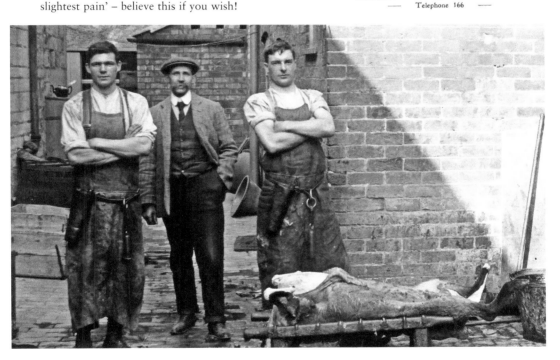

Butchers at Cainscross

This photograph is reported to have been taken behind The White Horse Inn at Cainscross. Curiously it shows butchers processing the carcass of a deer. Fixed to their belts are sheathes to hold knives and what I am told are implements for stunning animals prior to slaughter. Nowadays beasts would by law have to be taken to a registered abattoir.

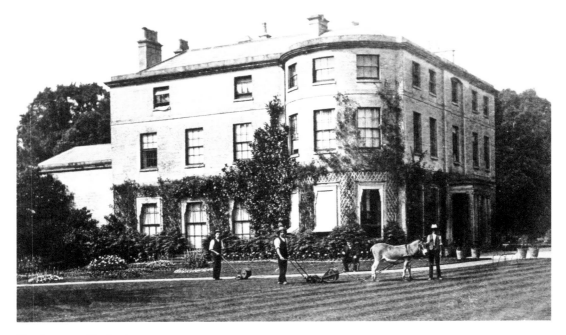

Gardeners at Eastington
In this mid-Edwardian scene at Eastington Park three gardeners mow the extensive lawns at the property. Could it perhaps be a comment on social rank at the time that the more senior gardener has a donkey to pull his machine, while the juniors have to push theirs? Or is it simply that smaller, hand-pushed mowers are better for edging?

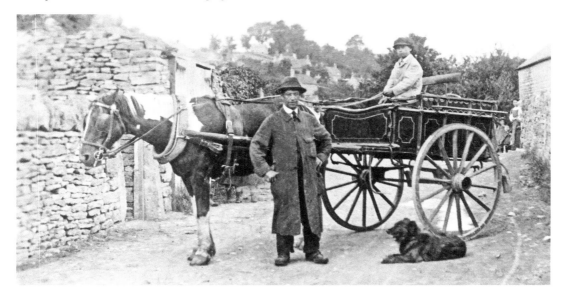

Milk Delivery at France Lynch
This is a scene that would have been common everywhere a century ago. According to information provided by the late Lionel Padin, the man in the foreground is Jack Liddiatt. His son Cyril is on the cart and the milk is from Williams's premises in Chalford High Street.

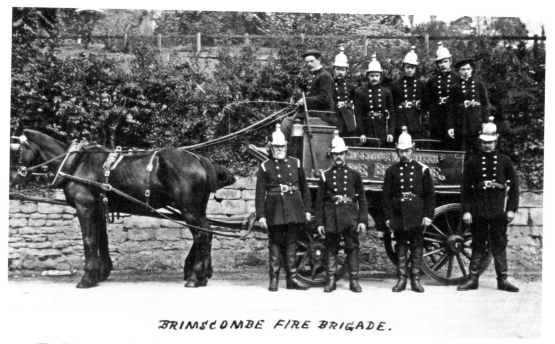

BRIMSCOMBE FIRE BRIGADE.

The Brimscombe Fire Brigade

Like other local villages such as Chalford, around 1900 Brimscombe had a horse-drawn, hand-pumped fire engine. At the time larger places such as Stroud were acquiring Merryweather steam-powered vehicles. Both of Stroud's brigades, the Volunteer and the Urban District Council, owned such a machine. In this picture the firemen have clearly polished their helmets, buttons and boots for the photographer's visit. The way he has cropped the image has unfortunately removed the end of the horse's nose.

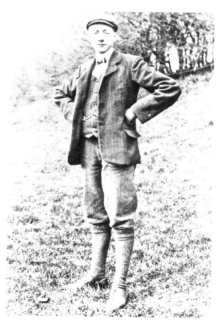

A Young Photographer

Today we snap away happily with smartphones. A century ago very few people owned cameras so, if a portrait or a picture of your house was required, you would visit one of the many local professionals. Stroud had several, one of whom was William Lee (1886–1965), a cousin of Laurie Lee. William's career began as soon as he left Marling School, where he is reputed to have acquired his photographic skills.

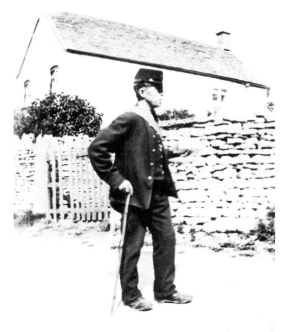

The Oakridge Postman

Born at Staunton around 1868, Sidney Barnett served the village of Oakridge for many years as its postman. In this view, preserved by a descendant, he is seen as a young man. His walking stick is more likely to have been used for warding off unfriendly dogs than for support. The photograph shows the uniform postmen wore a century ago.

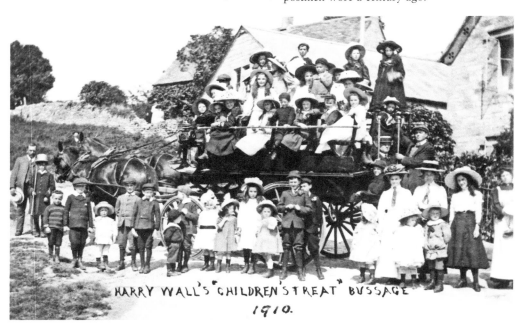

HARRY WALL'S "CHILDREN'S TREAT" BUSSAGE 1910.

Harry Wall's Children's Treat

Henry Wall (known as Harry) is listed in trade directories as the landlord of The Ram Inn at Bussage in 1910 and again in 1919. His children's treats were a feature of village life in the parish in the first part of the last century. Here an extremely heavily laden horse brake, packed with youngsters, is ready to set off from the pub. Harry's 1919 Trade Directory entry records him as publican, farmer, oil merchant and responsible for 'posting in all its branches.'

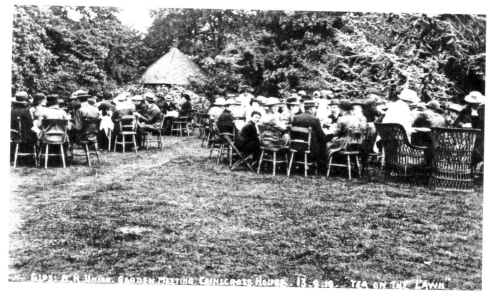

GLOS. B. H. UNION. GARDEN MEETING. CAINSCROSS HOUSE. 13.8.19. "TEA ON THE LAWN"

The Band of Hope

Founded as a reaction to the widespread misuse of alcohol in Victorian times, by 1900 the temperance movement was flourishing. My father, who was brought up at Bedford Street Congregational Chapel in Stroud, signed the pledge in 1915 to abstain from all alcohol. He faithfully kept his promise for forty years until he was finally persuaded to toast the happy pair at a family wedding in 1955! Here the Band of Hope Union enjoys a 1919 garden party at Cainscross House.

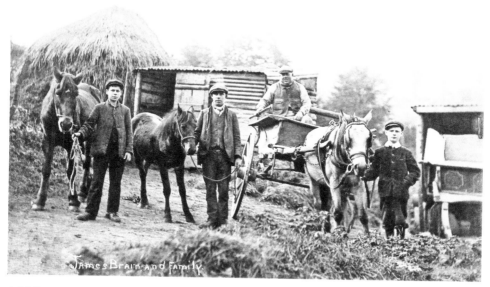

James Brain and Family

A Nailsworth Carrier's Business

James Brain was a carrier at Harley Wood, a hamlet near what is now Ruskin Mill in the Horsley Valley. He was apparently nicknamed 'Bully Brain', though the reason for this is not recorded. He was a general and agricultural carrier and is believed to have often transported lime for fertilising ploughed land.

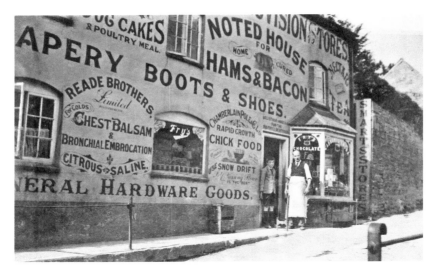

Mr Smart's General Store, Chalford
The Smart family were well known in Chalford a century ago. They ran a coal wharf on the Thames & Severn Canal, and also had a store in the High Street. The shop surely merits a prize for the most complete use of advertising space on a wall. The range of products shown is truly astonishing: drapery, boots and shoes, chest balsam, bronchial embrocation, pet food, hardware – the list is most impressive. The building remains, but its spectacular decoration is lost.

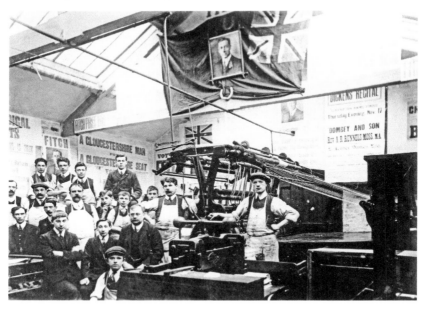

Inside the Stroud News Building
This is a fascinating picture of the inside of the office of one of Stroud's Edwardian newspapers. In 1910 – we know the date because Cecil Fitch was an election candidate in that year – Stroud had two local papers, the Conservative-supporting *News* and the *Journal*, whose allegiance was to the Liberal Party. The image shows an old way of producing an edition. A 1910 directory states that the *News* office was in George Street.

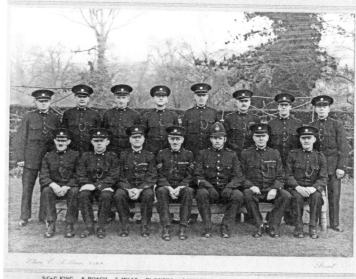

The Wartime Special Police

The 'Specials' played an invaluable role during the Second World War. The photograph shows the group attached to Rodborough parish.

My father is second from the right in the back row. During the day he worked on bullet machines at Hoffmann's factory in Stonehouse, then his night-time duties included aircraft watching from the tower of Rodborough Fort.

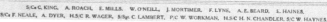

S/C° C. KING, A. ROACH, E. MILLS, W. O'NEILL, J. MORTIMER, F. LYNE, A. E. BEARD, E. HAINES.
S/C° F. NEALE, A. DYER, H.S/C R. WAGER, S/Sgt. C. LAMBERT, P/C W. WORKMAN, H.S/C H. N. CHANDLER, S/C W. HAYNES.

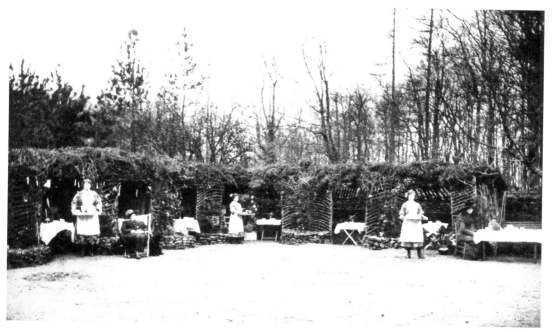

Miss Gardner, Teahouse Proprietor

For much of the early part of the last century Miss Gardner, later Mrs St. John, ran a popular teahouse close to Painswick Beacon, which offered accommodation as well as afternoon teas for locals and visitors. On fine days refreshments could be taken in the attractive setting of what one might perhaps call leafy arbours around her lawn.

POST CARD.

THE ADDRESS TO BE WRITTEN ON THIS SIDE.

MRS. ST. JOHN
(*née* MISS GARDNER)
Castle Bungalow,
PAINSWICK HILL, STROUD, GLOS.

Paying Guests' House on 18-hole Golf Course.
Green, 5 minutes.

TEA GARDENS open all the year round.
MOTOR BUSES pass hourly—Gloucester, Stroud,
Cheltenham.
GOLF CHARGES : **1/6** per day, **7/6** per week, **20/-** per
month, for Visitors, who will find the Links unsurpassed
for beauty of situation and bracing air—elevation 800 feet.

Telegrams : "ST. JOHN, BUNGALOW, PAINSWICK."

The Teahouse Advertisement

Mrs St. John's advertising card mentions the golf course five minutes away (daily charge 1s 6d) and adds that access is easily available to Castle Bungalow by motor buses that pass hourly.

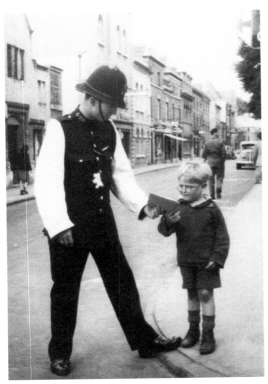

The Policeman at the Town Time

Back in 1946, traffic in High Street, King Street, Gloucester Street and Lansdown was two way, requiring a policeman wearing white traffic sleeves to stand where these streets meet. However, the picture of Sgt Norman Stevens has a story accompanying it. Whenever Norman was working, a young evacuee from London used to wait for him to come off duty, then proudly rush to show him his schoolwork. The boy's name is not known, but it's a rather touching story.

6

Events

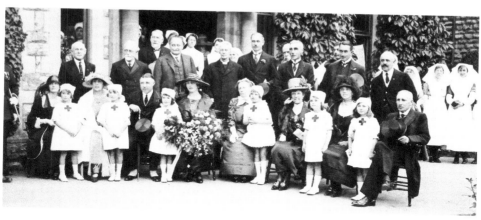

A Princess's Visit

Stroud Hospital was built in 1873. By the end of the First World War improvements were needed and the new Peace Memorial Wing was put up fronting Trinity Road. This involved the loss of the west end of the original building. The new extension was opened on 6 July 1922 by Princess Alice of Athlone. She is seen here outside the main entrance with a group of local dignitaries including Sir Percival and Lady Marling.

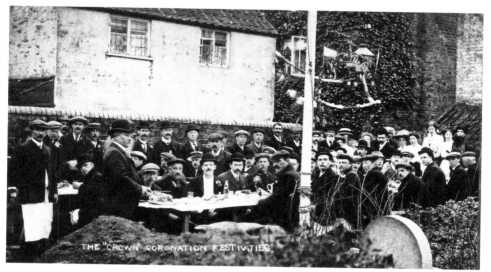

Coronation Festivities at Ebley

Events such as coronations and royal weddings are still marked with celebrations today, but what makes this photograph reminiscent of a vanished world is that all those seated for the 1911 coronation feast are male. The few ladies present appear to be there purely to serve the meal.

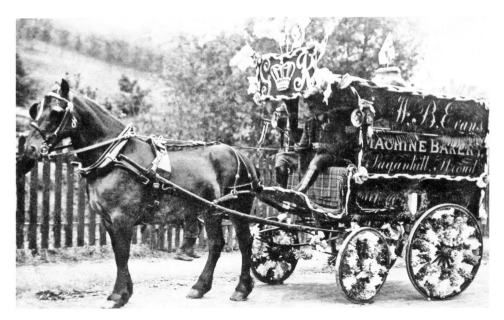

A Coronation Carnival

Carnival processions celebrating major events were often extensive affairs with participants both in vehicles and on foot. Mr Evans of Paganhill clearly went to some trouble to decorate his bread delivery van in an appropriate way for the occasion in 1911.

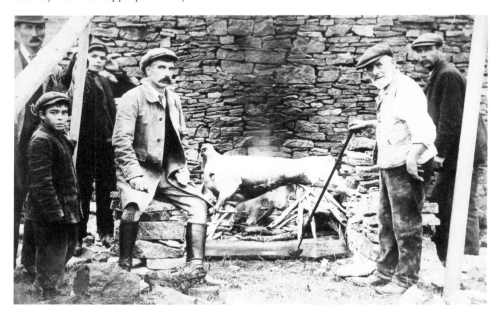

The Bisley Coronation Sheep Roast

In this attractive picture of the Bisley sheep roast note how heavily dressed everyone is – even the person charged with tending the roasting carcass has only removed his coat, although it's a June day. A century ago hats and jackets were considered almost de rigeur, whatever the season or the temperature.

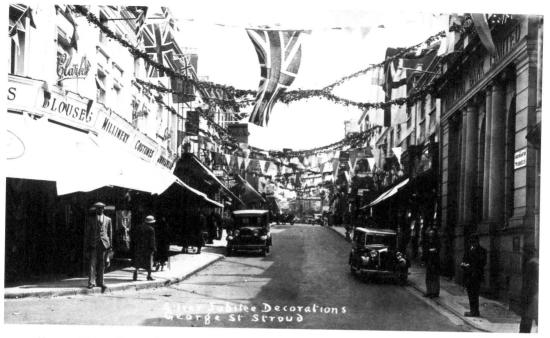

Above and below: George V's 1935 Silver Jubilee

Nowadays towns and villages are rarely decorated for special occasions anywhere near as comprehensively as used to be the case. Also flags and bunting were then generally provided by businesses and private individuals, not local councils. On this page we see two pictures of Stroud as it looked at the time of George V and Queen Mary's Silver Jubilee in 1935. Both are by Rodborough photographer William Adams.

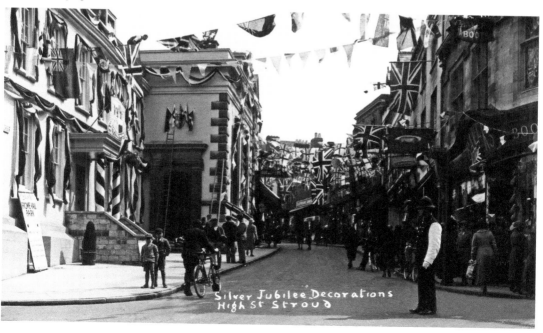

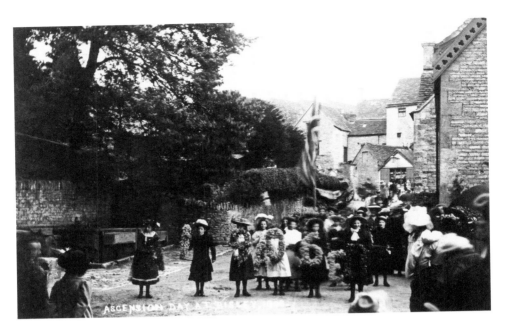

Dressing the Wells, Bisley

The clothing of those taking part in the annual Ascension Day ceremony is so different today. In 1906 the children were dressed as miniature versions of their elders, whereas nowadays they wear school uniform with the exception of the main flower bearers who are in Bluecoat School costumes.

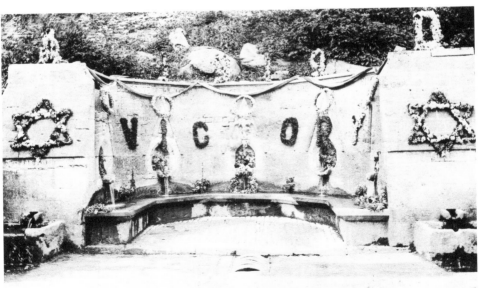

The 1919 Wells Dressing

In the Ascension Day ritual of 1919, organisers of the event clearly felt that the general relief experienced following the end of the First World War hostilities required that the main word spelt out in flowers should be changed to 'VICTORY' rather than 'ASCENSION', as was normal.

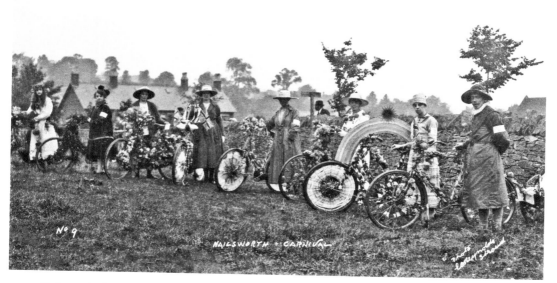

Nailsworth Carnival

Most carnivals a century ago would have been more extensive occasions than those today. A popular theme was the decorated bicycle competition, not usually a feature of present-day events. This is almost certainly the Nailsworth carnival of 1921.

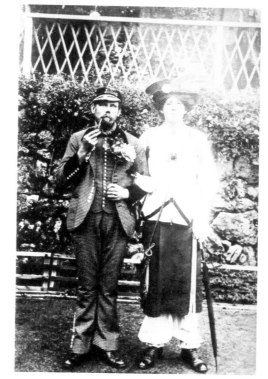

Two Characters

Men 100 years ago often dressed as women for carnivals. The photograph shows two Stroud businessmen in festive mood. On the left is my great-uncle Henry Thomas Pearce, who ran a blacksmith's business in London Road. With him is Frank Ford, son of builder and undertaker Philip Ford.

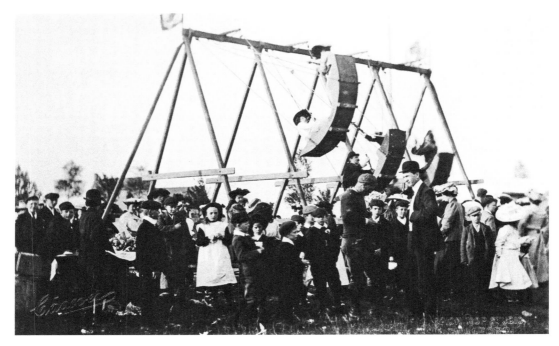

Swingboats

Nowadays swingboats are not as regular a feature in fêtes as they once were. Around 1910 an unknown photographer captured this scene in the children's playground at Chalford Hill. What seems curious is that all the 'boats' are in focus. Was this luck, or did he take multiple pictures of the children and then select for his postcard the only one that wasn't blurred?

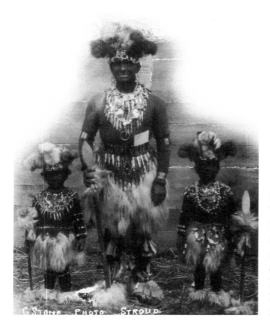

Stroud's Most Extroverted Showman

Vincent 'Spot' Walker, who ran an early cinema in Lansdown, has dressed here as an African native to encourage youngsters along to his show. He is accompanied by two young volunteers, liberally covered in what was probably boot polish. He called them Timbuc One and Timbuc Two! No one has emerged over the last century to match 'Spot' for sheer showmanship.

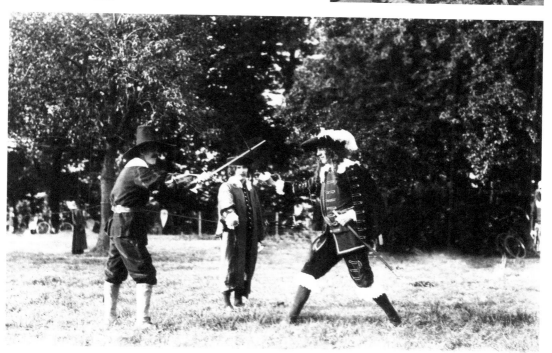

The Great Pageant of 1911

An event that has never been repeated on anywhere near the same scale was the splendid 1911 Mid-Gloucestershire Historical Pageant of Progress. A cast of 1,100 took part; the show lasted two and a half hours, with a script entirely in rhyming couplets. It was staged in the open air at Fromehall Park. Different parts of the Stroud district represented different periods in history. Here a participant from the Stonehouse area is imaginatively dressed as an ancient British warrior.

Civil War Bicycles

Painswick and nearby villages covered the Civil War period in the 1911 pageant. Here a roundhead and a cavalier pose for a duel. Note, however, the photographer's unsuccessful attempt to erase bicycles parked in the background!

71

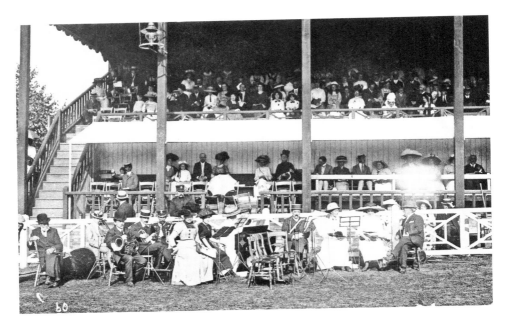

The Pageant Orchestra

This photograph, which only came to light very recently, shows the orchestra that accompanied the various songs in the pageant. Being out of doors, it was fortunate that no performance took place in bad weather. The structure in the background is Stroud Rugby Club's grandstand.

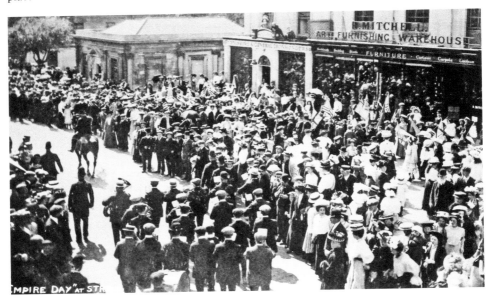

Empire Day at Stroud

Each 24 May, on Empire Day, Edwardian schoolchildren would be formed into a gigantic procession to march from the centre of Stroud to Fromehall Park. Also included would be the town's two fire engines. Head of Stroud's police force, Supt Biggs, is seen here on horseback in the procession, followed by a band. Today the concept of empire is rather politically incorrect. Edwardians harboured no such sentiments.

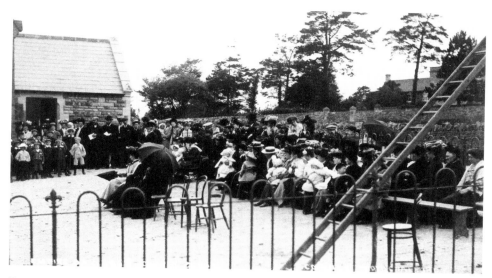

Empire Day at Chalford

In local villages Empire Day was celebrated in more modest, but no less enthusiastic, ways. Here at Chalford Hill School we see the festivities for 1908. The children on the left are lined up ready to recite or sing. Parents and visitors look on. It's an interesting comment on the social etiquette of the period that persons of note are allocated special seating separate from the rest of the crowd.

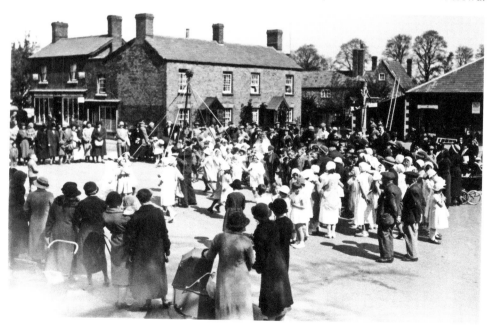

May Day at Eastington

Of all the villages in the area Eastington was the most enthusiastic in its celebration of May Day. This was largely due to the school's headmaster, Mr John Rowbottom. A senior girl was always chosen as May Queen. She was supported by two smaller girl attendants and two boys in pseudo-eighteenth-century costume. The picture shows villagers watching maypole dancing at The Cross.

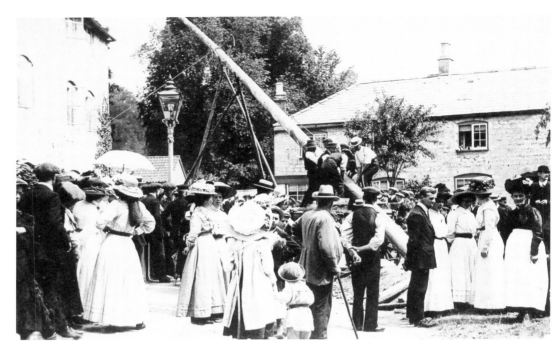

The Paganhill Maypole

A maypole has stood at Paganhill since at least 1804 and is a well-known local landmark. Occasionally it needs taking down for maintenance work or replacement. The photograph probably shows its re-erection on 5 June 1911 at the time of the coronation of George V and Queen Mary. The image is unposed and pleasing since almost no one has noticed the presence of the photographer. The maypole survives today, but the method of erection shown here has mercifully been superseded.

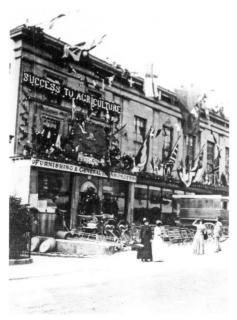

The 1892 Visit of the County Agricultural Show

When Stroud's turn came to host visits by the County Agricultural Show, as happened several times before the First World War, no expense was spared in decorating the town. This image from 1892 comes from a rare magic lantern plate and shows the building that later became Woolworths in King Street Parade. On the right can be seen Spratt's horse bus, which served the Stonehouse area.

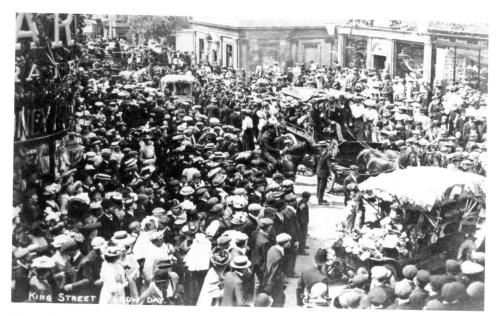

The 1907 County Agricultural Show Visit

Five highly decorated arches were put up in the town for the 1907 visit of the County Show. They were basically wooden structures hung with material, flags, bunting and greenery. Over the Gloucester Street arch was a medallion carrying the words 'Speed the Plough'. The show included a decorated vehicle competition. Participants are seen here in King Street.

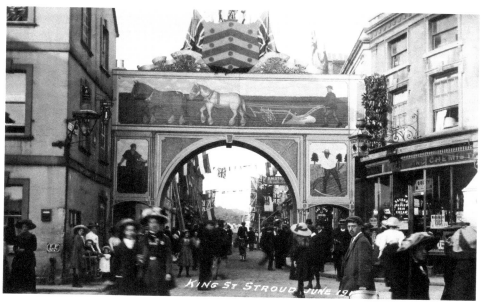

The 1912 County Agricultural Show Visit

Re-erected five years later, the King Street arch was the most complicated and carefully crafted of the five. It was put together by local builder Philip Ford and on its panels were painted representations of ploughing, sowing and reaping. There is evidence that this structure was later borrowed for use in Cirencester.

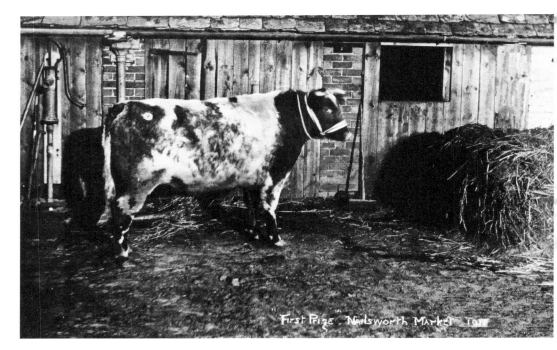

A Prize Beast

Old Market in Nailsworth now includes the library, the bus station, the Mortimer Room, the tourist information office, several shops and a car park. It now acts as a through route to Cossack Square. A century ago it was the location for a cattle market where animals were exhibited and sold. Local photographer E. P. Conway took this picture of the beast judged to be the finest in its class in 1911. According to a local farming expert the cow is a Dairy Shorthorn.

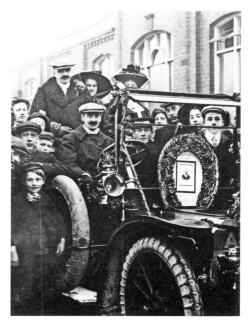

Charles Allen, Liberal MP

From 1900 to 1918 Liberal MP Charles P. Allen represented the Stroud constituency. My father, a boy at the time, recalled many rousing renditions of the Liberal election song 'Roll on Charlie Allen'. I remember him still singing snatches of it in the 1970s. Standing in the car, Mr Allen is seen here electioneering in friendly territory at Dudbridge.

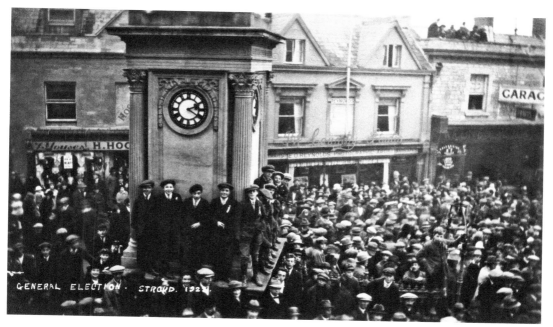

Electioneering in Stroud

Much of the boisterous, sometimes overtly physical, behaviour that accompanied elections a hundred years ago has happily been lost. At Stroud, in the days before the advent of public media, election results were announced in daylight from the balcony of the Subscription Rooms. Sizeable crowds waited all around. The photograph shows the time leading up to the declaration of poll for the 1922 general election. Conservative candidate Stanley Tubbs achieved a majority of over 5,000.

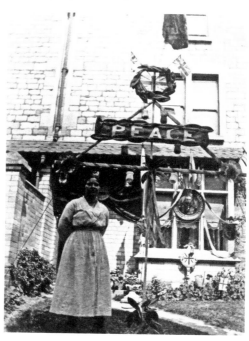

Peace Day, 1919

The day chosen for the national commemoration of the ending of the First World War was 19 July 1919. For some it was merely a time to resume the pre-war carnivals and fêtes which had been so much a feature of the first years of the century. For many others, who had lost relatives or close friends, Peace Day must have been more a time of mixed feelings. The photograph shows a house at Ebley decorated for the occasion.

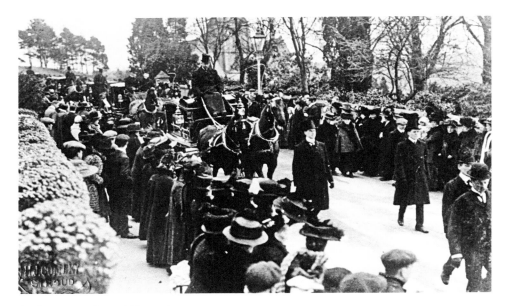

An Important Stroud Funeral

This image shows the funeral arranged for Sir John Dorington of Lypiatt Park, who died on 5 April 1911. In the photograph the cortege, with its horse-drawn hearse, has arrived at the cemetery in Bisley Road. Crowds of respectful onlookers, several deep in places, line the pavement. Everyone of importance in the Stroud area would have been present.

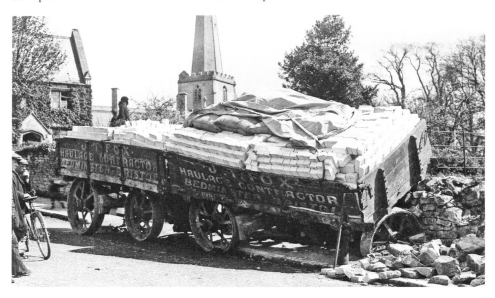

An Accident at Painswick

The exact date of the photograph is not known. It records an industry once common in the area. Stone quarrying on Painswick Beacon had taken place for centuries. Here a heavily laden vehicle owned by J. T. Fox, haulier of Bristol, has come to grief in the centre of Painswick. One can only speculate as to the cause, but the wagon may have been overloaded. The event must have caused quite a stir in the town.

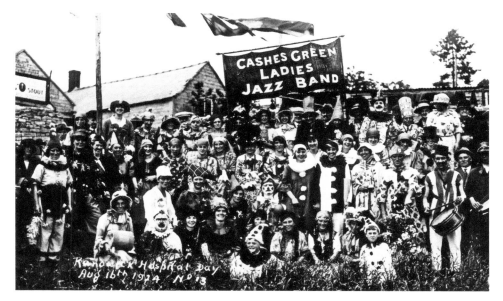

Jazz Bands

During the interwar years local jazz bands were popular, and were formed both in villages and in factories such as Holloways in Stroud. Members enjoyed dressing up and playing relatively simple instruments. The picture shows the Cashes Green Ladies Jazz Band taking part in the Randwick Hospital Day Carnival of August 1924. Also in the procession was the Whiteshill and Ruscombe Brass Band. The event included bowling for a live pig and a competition guessing how long a candle would burn.

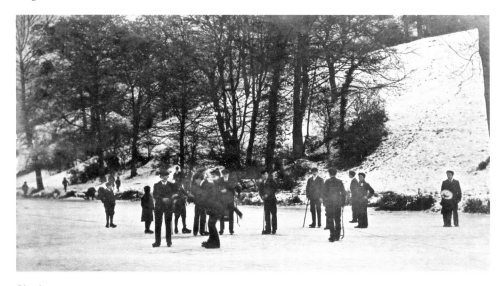

Skating

Skating on lakes and millponds was an Edwardian pastime that has largely disappeared. One reason is that nowadays we do not often experience the really cold winters that were common to our forebears. Another is that today Health and Safety regulations would disapprove – and probably rightly so. This view of Toadsmoor Lake dates from January 1905.

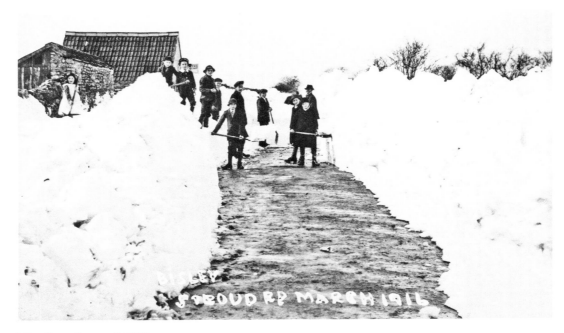

The Great Snow of 1916

The winter of 1915–16 was unusual. Mild January temperatures had resulted in spring flowers blossoming, but late February saw a dramatic change. What was described in the local press as 'the heaviest snowfall for a generation' particularly affected Bisley. Frederick Major produced a series of spectacular postcards recording what his village looked like and especially how the weather had affected access roads into it.

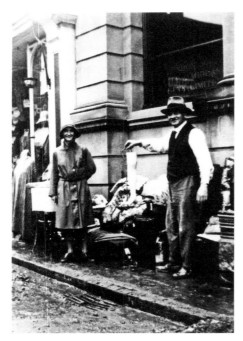

Floods at Nailsworth

People today remember the 2007 flood as being severe. However, largely lost to memory is another that was even more spectacular. In August 1931 a thunderstorm struck Nailsworth. Torrential rain lasting for five hours resulted in surface water from surrounding valleys converging in the centre of the town. A shopfront was washed away and four sheep survived only by climbing onto their manger. Locals pulled hams and bacon from the mud to take home. The photograph shows damaged property from commercial premises in George Street.

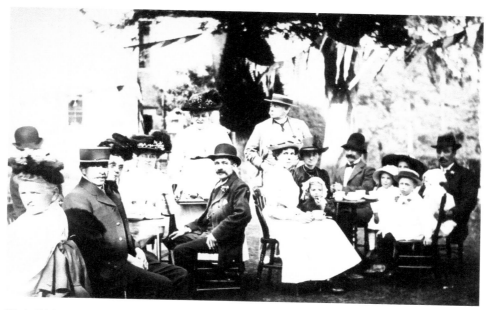

Little Did They Know

In July 1914 Major Drummond (standing) hosted a garden party at his home, The Chantry at Bisley. Those seated at the tables look serious. However, they would have looked even more so had they suspected the magnitude of the tragedy that would befall England within the next month: the onset of the First World War. The settled life of Edwardian England would be gone forever.

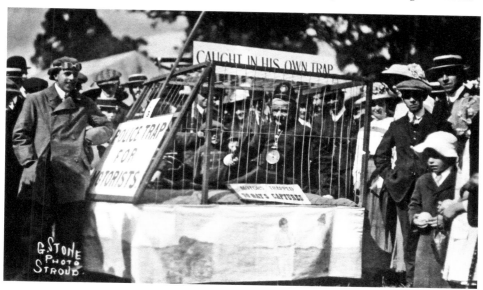

A Police Speed Trap

Today a police speed trap involves a camera, either hand held or, more often, mounted in one of the familiar yellow roadside boxes. People a century ago clearly felt as annoyed as many do today when caught for minor offences. The idea of getting one's own back on the law appealed to someone around 1910 when planning what theme to use for a carnival float. The result is an amusing postcard.

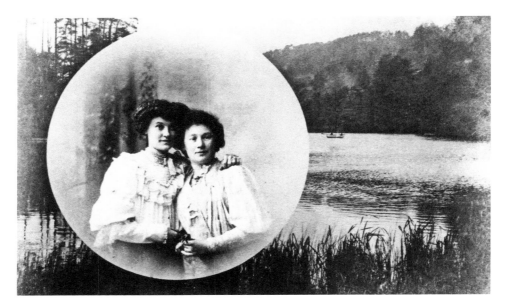

Woodchester Lakes

Woodchester Park, with its series of lakes, was freely accessible a hundred years ago. I know my grandmother spent happy days there – well worth the walk from Nailsworth. However, during my own youth the chance of seeing this beautiful valley was lost to all but a few. Now, happily, the valley and the mansion are open to visitors once again. Here an enterprising Edwardian photographer has used a lake view as the background for a studio portrait.

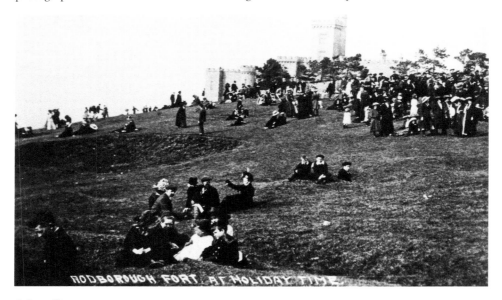

A Lost Custom

On fine summer weekends during the early years of the last century the hillside below Rodborough Fort would fill with people, just sitting, walking, or simply taking the air. For Stroud folk, most of whom lacked transport, this was an easy spot to reach to meet friends or take a picnic. The photograph was taken around 1905.

7
Children

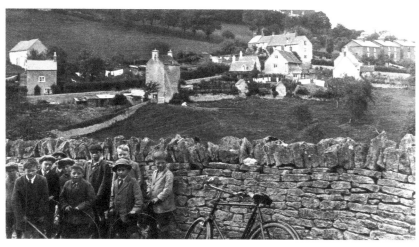

Butterrow Boys

The boys here really bring to life what would otherwise have been a rather uninteresting image. It seems probable that a photographer was passing the little school at Butterrow – now a private house – when schoolchildren were emerging, so he took his opportunity to include them in the picture. Note the metal hoops and sticks for bowling them. Also note the jackets, ties and caps the boys are wearing in what is clearly not a winter scene.

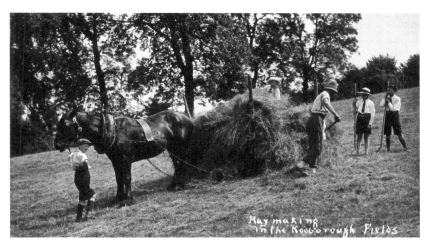

Helping in the Fields

Children in the 1920s generally played a part in the seasonal activity of haymaking. Here in Rodborough fields quite young boys assist in loading hay onto what appears to be a kind of sledge. Two with pitchforks have helped to move the hay; one steadies the horse while a fourth is on top.

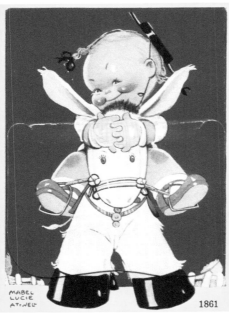

You can see I'm Enjoying Meself at STROUD

'Enjoying Meself at Stroud'

For much of the last century Mabel Lucie Atwell's cartoon postcards were popular. Born in 1879, she died in 1964. Around 1914 Mabel developed her trademark style of sentimentalised chubby children. The cards were often overprinted with the name of the town where they were intended to be sold. The flap covering the donkey's body lifts up and, in concertina form, twelve local views appear.

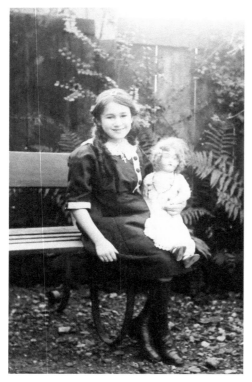

Buttoned Boots

Ruby Court, a teacher and amateur artist, lived for many years in Nelson Street, Stroud. She is seen here around 1920 pictured with her doll. This image is included because it shows the sort of boots girls wore in the early part of the last century. A button hook would have been needed to fasten and unfasten them.

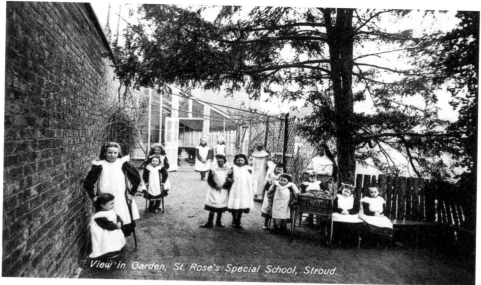

View in Garden, St. Rose's Special School, Stroud.

St Rose's Special School

Early last century a girl with special needs was brought to the Dominican Sisters at St Rose's Convent in Stroud. This led to the founding of the Special School in 1912. The photograph was taken sometime in the school's early years and shows both how the girls were dressed and also that nuns then worked in full habit. In 1973 the school held a sponsored silence to raise funds for Mother Teresa, who actually visited later that year.

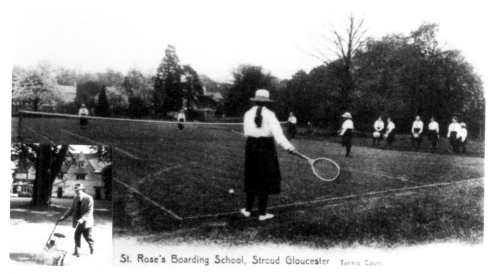

St. Rose's Boarding School, Stroud Gloucester Tennis Court.

Tennis Outfits

A girls' private Catholic school – St Rose's Convent – also existed for many years at Stroud. It was founded in the early 1920s, closed somewhere around 1970 and its main building (seen in the background of the inset image with gardener Fred Gibbons mowing the lawn) was subsequently demolished. The photograph shows how the girls were expected to dress for tennis in the 1920s. Hats, stockings and skirts below the knee were still the norm for physical activities.

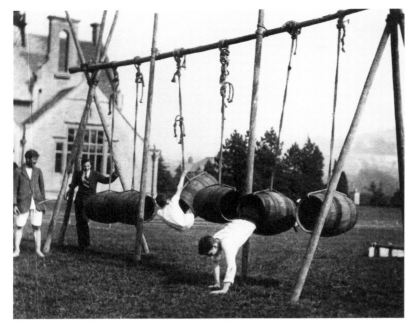

A Barrel of Fun
Here an obstacle race at Marling School is taking place around 1920. The picture is part of a series of postcards, all apparently taken on the same occasion. The image is included because nowadays Health and Safety regulations would be sure to forbid pupils climbing through barrels.

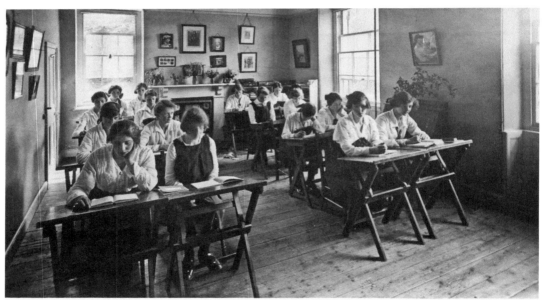

⁵¹047   Bussage House. Gloucestershire. Fifth Form Room.   (COPYRIGHT)
P. A. BUCHANAN & Co.
CROYDON.

Bussage House School

Bussage House was home to John Sibree's boys' school in the nineteenth century, but it had closed before 1912 when the property was opened as a girls' school by Dorothea Beale, niece of the Miss Beale who founded Cheltenham Ladies' College. Note the folding desks, which could easily be stacked away when the room was to be used for drama or other lessons requiring space. The building is now a private house.

8

Rural Life

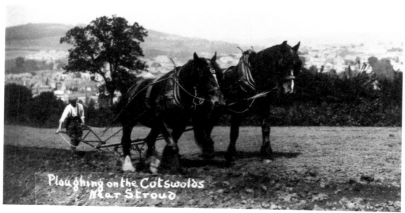

Horse Ploughing at Rodborough

Horses such as these were commandeered in 1914 to haul gun carriages. For us in twenty-first-century England it is hard to believe that this scene was commonplace, especially on smaller farms, until around the Second World War. How fortunate that photographer William Adams, who only lived a few yards away, felt it was worth recording. This image represents a timeless picture of a rural way of life, which has vanished except at staged country life events.

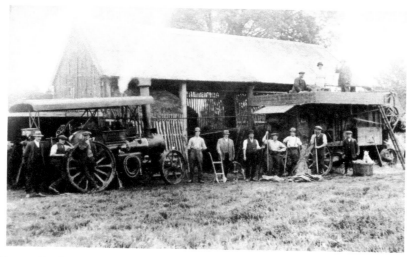

Threshing at Eastington

Here again is a rural scene once familiar yet now remembered only by the elderly. The picture was taken at Warner's Farm at Eastington. Sheaves stored in the barn are being threshed using a machine made by Marshalls of Gainsborough, which is linked to a traction engine owned by Browning Brothers of Stonehouse. The photograph dates from around 1920.

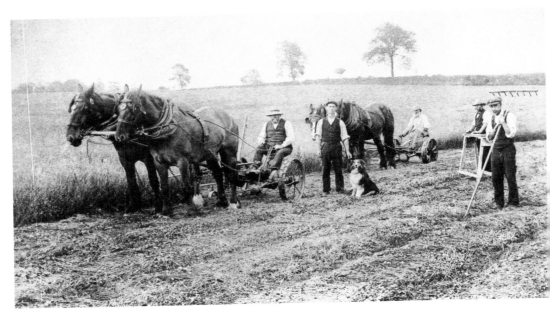

Mowing at Bisley

Who took this well-focused mowing picture is unknown. Meadow grass is being cut with a pair of simple mowing machines. The man on the right is thought to be in charge of a whetstone mounted on a small table. This would have made it unnecessary to return to the farm when the mowing blades needed sharpening.

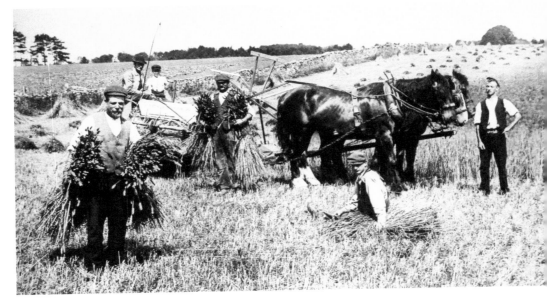

Cutting the Corn

This Bisley photograph is one of the very finest local rural life images to have survived. It dates from around 1910. Bisley photographer Frederick Major produced hundreds of real photographs as postcards – all unsigned. In addition he issued a second series of printed postcards that bear his name, but lack the definition of his photographic ones.

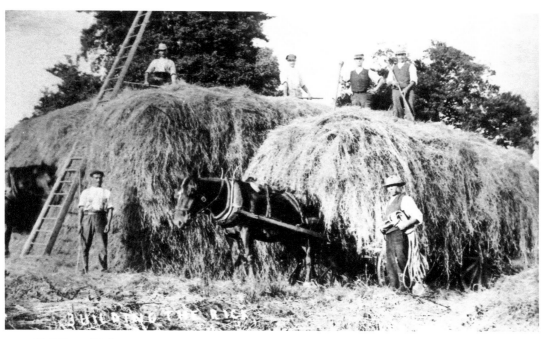

Building a Rick

An equally atmospheric though slightly faded image by Major shows the construction of a large hayrick. The location is again likely to be Bisley. Note the quantity of hay arriving on the horse-drawn wagon and the length of the ladder needed for such a potentially high structure.

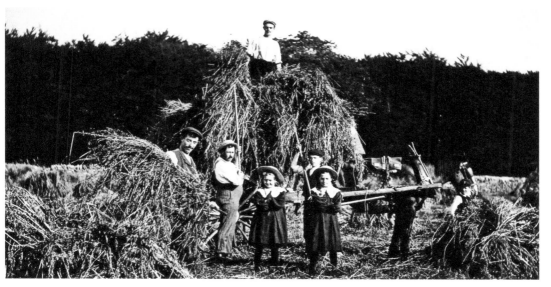

Harvesting at Brimscombe

The charm of this pastoral image lies partly in the children in the foreground, though whether they were dressed for work in the fields is questionable. The picture is linked to Brimscombe only by its postmark, dated 2 October 1907. Any information as to who the people are would be gratefully received.

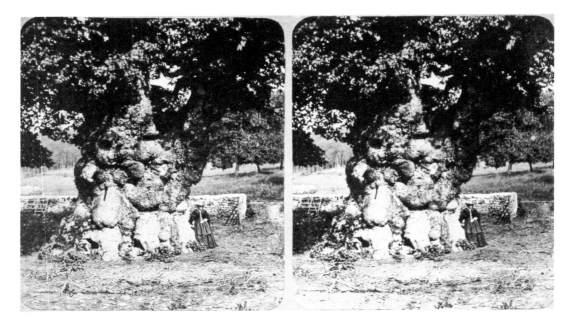

The Giant Elm

This curious stereoscopic card is intended to be seen through a 3D viewer. It is one of the very earliest known countryside photographs of the Stroud area. It is dated March 1860. A comparison with a watercolour in the Museum in the Park suggests that it may well have been situated at Abbey Farm in the hamlet of The Vatch. Already clearly ancient, it would probably have disappeared by the end of the nineteenth century.

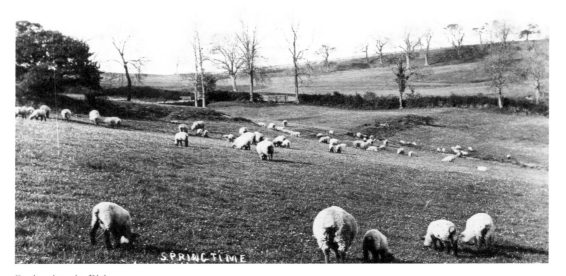

Springtime in Bisley

This charming rural life postcard was sent in September 1910 by someone signing himself George, to a Miss A. Davis, and includes the words 'I am in Bisley with Ethel. This is a postcard of the field where we picked the watercress.' Country people in Edwardian days relied much more on gathering freely available wild produce from hedgerows, woods and meadows than is common today.

9

The Landscape

Over the years, housing developments – often extensive – have resulted in the disappearance of many green spaces once part of the district's landscape.

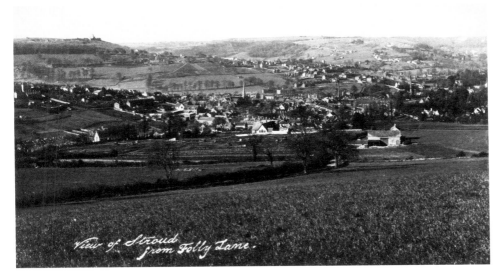

Above and below: Stroud from Folly Lane
Photographs a century apart taken at the top of Folly Lane show the extent of building development at Uplands and, more distantly, at Rodborough.

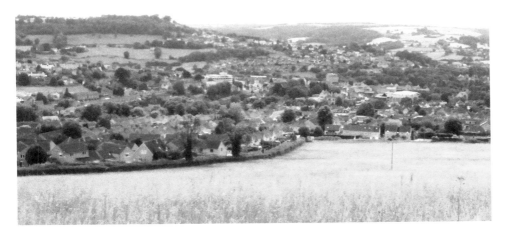

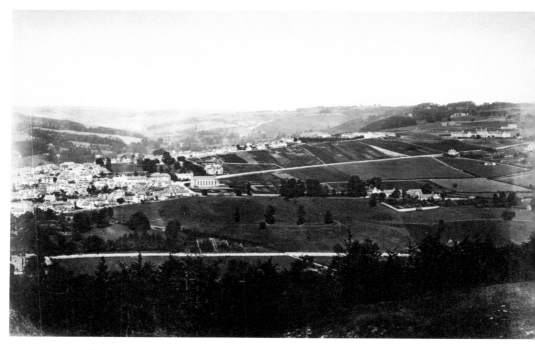

Above and below: Upper Stroud from Rodborough Fort

The early image, taken from near Rodborough Fort, is from 1870 with almost no houses along London Road, Bowbridge Lane or Bisley Road. Park Road doesn't exist. The present-day photograph was taken from Butterrow Lane, since tree growth prevents an exact match with the view of a century and a half ago.

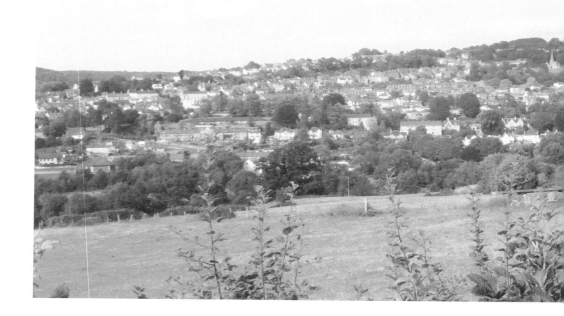

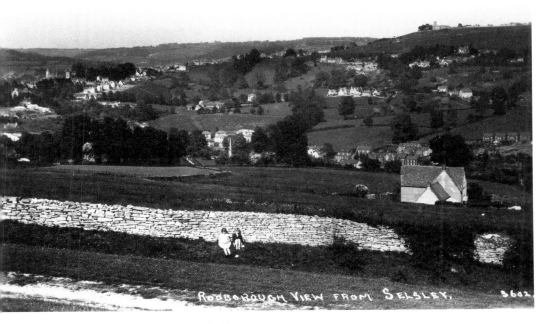

Above and below: Rodborough from Selsley

Here it has been possible to stand almost exactly where the interwar years picture was taken from Selsley Hill.

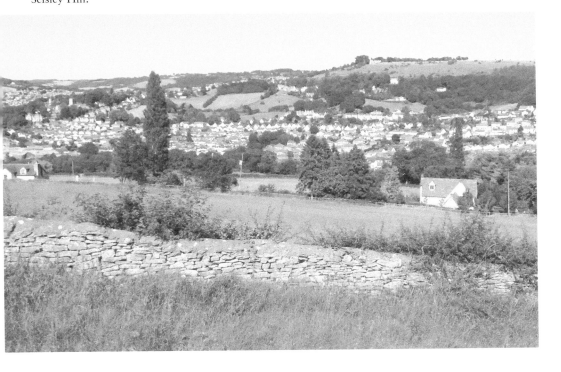

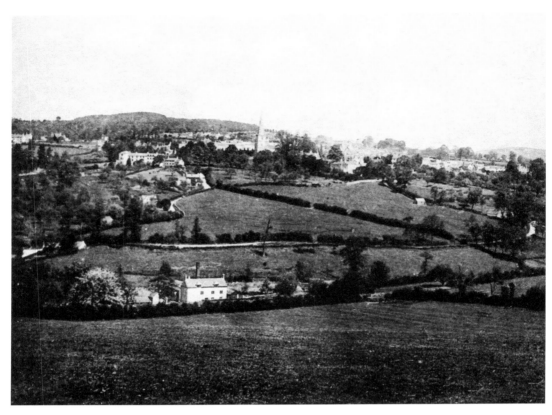

Above and below: Painswick from Stepping Stone Lane
The early view of Painswick was taken in the 1890s. It shows almost none of the buildings later put up on the lower side of the town.

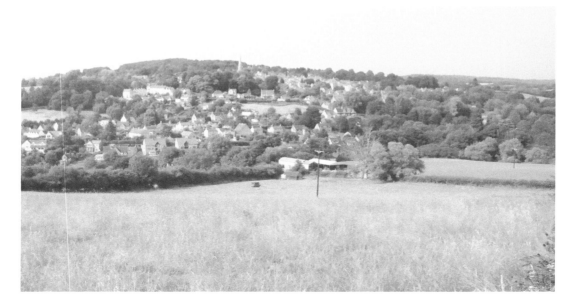

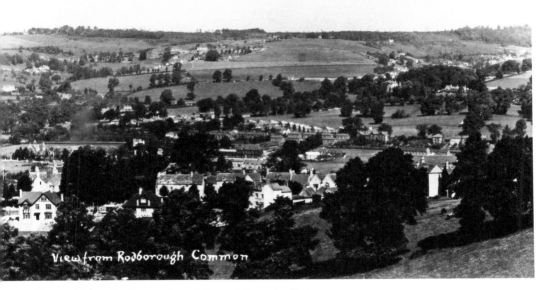

Above and below: Rodborough and Beyond from the Fort
Photographer William Adams took this 1920s view from the old trackway below Rodborough Fort. The buildings on Walkley Hill in the foreground are largely unaltered. What is noticeable is the extensive change to landscape in the distance.

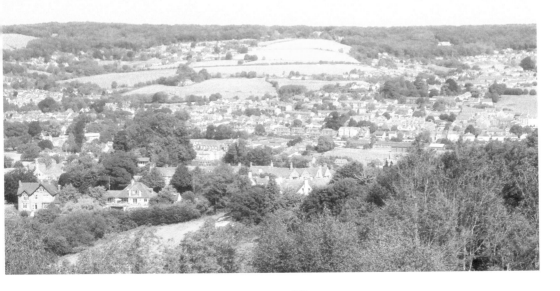

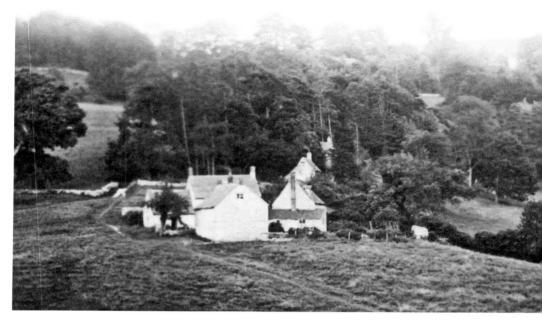

Weyhouse
The final photograph is actually a reversal of the process seen in this chapter. Here, what was a century ago a small hamlet on the hillside east of Bowbridge has now completely disappeared and reverted to grassland. The site of Weyhouse is approached by taking the footpath down the side of the lower part of Stroud Cemetery, crossing the stream and climbing the slope beyond.

Acknowledgements

Mrs B. Barnfield, Ms A. Blick, Mr J. Curtis, Mrs K. Edwards, Mr M. Fenton, Mr C. Field, Mr M. Gibbons, Mr P. Griffin, Mrs M. Griffiths, Mr P. Harris, Miss M. Hodges, Mr D. Ireland, Mr D. Jowett, Mrs D. Martin, Mr D. Nathan, Mr H. Neale, Ms D. Odell, Mr A. Peyton, Mrs J. Taylor, Mrs M. Tyler, Mr P. Walker, Ms V. Walker, Mr L. Walrond and Mr R. Young.
  Special thanks to my wife, Sylvia, for all her assistance in preparing this book.